THE RIVER IS HERE

Receiving And Sustaining The Blessing Of Revival

Melinda Fish

Melinda Fish

OTHER BOOKS BY THIS AUTHOR

When Addiction Comes To Church, later published as I Can't Be An Addict I'm A Christian

Adult Children And The Almighty

Restoring The Wounded Woman

I'm So Tired of Acting Spiritual: Peeling Back The Mask

The River Is Here (1st Edition)

Keep Coming, Holy Spirit!

The Accidental Intercessor: The Supernatural Power of an Ordinary Life

What readers say-

John Arnott, Founder of Catch the Fire- (From the foreword)

" If you want to prepare yourself for the next great move of God, then this book will answer most of your concerns, and generate in you a great hunger and love for more of Him which is His Holy Spirit's promise to you. Hopefully it will restore a deep first love passion for Jesus Christ your Saviour, Lord and soon returning King…"

Dr. R. T. Kendall, theologian, author of the upcoming *PROPHETIC INTEGRITY* (from the foreword to this book)

"…I recommend Melinda Fish's book to be read far and wide. Read it with an open mind. If you have been a critic of this phenomenon, it could be you are in for the surprise of your life."

Stuart Bell, Pastor, Alive Church, Lincoln, England

" I'm honoured to endorse the updated version of THE RIVER IS HERE. On reading the manuscript, I was taken back into some of the most exciting and rewarding days of my life so far. I had the privilege of witnessing first hand some of the amazing activity of the Holy Spirit and the outpouring of God's love. Wonderful stories need to be recorded and recounted by gifted story tellers. There is no one who could both accurately and sensitively share these stories better than my good friend, Melinda Fish. She has been uniquely placed by God to give testimony to one of the greatest moves of God in our time.

Pastor John Crane, Evangelistic Center Church, Shawnee, KS

"If you are hungry to understand how the Holy Spirit moves in revival and want to be personally positioned to receive the current move of the Holy Spirit, this book by Melinda Fish, The River is Here will challenge and guide you into experiencing revival. It gives you a new understanding of how God has moved in previous times and prepares you for what God is going to do next." Pastor John Crane, The Evangelistic Center Church, Shawnee Kansas. (Grandson of A.J. Rowden, chapter 11)

Dr. Eddie Hyatt, church historian, author

"*The River is Here* by Melinda Fish is a captivating personal account of her journey into genuine Holy Spirit revival. The personal stories will inspire you and the Bible-based exhortations will help you correct your course and stay in the middle of the River. This is a must read for those hungering after genuine, God-sent revival in the 21st century."

Pastors Wes and Sharron Boxall
Golden Valley Church, Gloucester, UK
In September 2019 my wife, Sharron, and I were driving our dear friends Melinda and Bill Fish between venues on their visit to England. During our journey I asked Melinda if she'd of re-publishing her book, THE RIVER IS HERE. I remember her saying that others had asked her the same question. How excited we are therefore, that she has done it!.

As I've read throught the pages, I've laughed and cried. I've remembered and been deeply stirred within. The wisdom contained within these pages is rare.

Melinda is the real deal, and this book is one of heaven's true gems. With all my heart I believe this reprint to be most timely. In looking back we are enabled to also look ahead. This is a book for the heart. It is able to assist us in guarding and sustaining what God did before, and in preparing and positioning us for what He wants to do next. I am truly thankful that, THE RIVER IS HERE, is here again. May you be blessed as you read it.

Dedication

I dedicate this new edition of THE RIVER IS HERE
to
every person spiritually hungry enough to open their lives to
the moving of the Holy Spirit
regardless of the cost.
May you be filled "with all the fullness of God."
Ephesians 3:19
- Melinda Fish

FOREWORD

by John Arnott

2021

I first became acquainted with Melinda when I received her manuscript in the mail for the first edition of this book back in 1995. I loved the book and called her immediately. It was the work of a skillful writer with clever, humorous and astounding reports and insights of what the Holy Spirit was doing in her personal family life, friends, and in her church.

I was soon to meet Melinda and her husband William (Bill) Fish on their next trip to Toronto. (They visited the Toronto Blessing revival more than 100 times, and she was soon to become the editor of our *Spread the Fire* magazine that we sent out bimonthly.) We became and still are to this day, really good friends. All of us are a bit older and hopefully quite a bit wiser now, and it is very appropriate that Melinda would undertake a major revision of her original work, that will prove to be very helpful to so many who are looking for teaching, advice and counsel regarding how to prepare for what God is about to do on the earth as he pours out his Holy Spirit in unprecedented manners and measures.

She is a very capable and gifted writer, and an excellent communicator who has been responsible for several 'revival' aphorisms, such as, *"There are no toxic levels of the Holy Spirit!"This new edition of The River Is Here is revised and updated. It is a compelling apologetic for the revival known as the Toronto Blessing, but goes well beyond that by presenting a comprehensive biblical preparation for the imminent global outpouring of the power of the Holy Spirit, that actually has already begun.*

Melinda Fish, originally from Texas, and a high school English teacher by profession, ended up in pastoral ministry because of the impact of the charismatic revival in the 70's that swept her and her husband Bill into its wonderful refreshing. That led them ultimately into pastoring in Pittsburgh Pennsylvania, USA where they continue ministering to this day.

This book will grip you and cause you to consider- or reconsider- the invaluable benefit of being filled yet again with God the Holy Spirit. *(Eph.5:18)*.

It is amazing to me to see how the Word and the Spirit always must go together. We desperately need them both, and of course the Holy Spirit, through 40 different authors, wrote the Word of God. Melinda does an excellent job of explaining how biblical it is to have powerful life-changing encounters with the Holy Spirit, and how subsequently, we are required to stay true to the boundaries, principles and teachings of the Word of God while at the same time, fully surrendering and yielding to the Spirit of God.

If you happen to be one who missed the revival in the 90's and the 2000's, then this edition will help explain how or why that happened. Perhaps you were fearful, or dissuaded by well-meaning friends, or even put off by the intensity of the manifestations and the zeal of affected believers. Or perhaps you just never heard about it. But she explains also how you might well have missed the greatest blessing of your entire lifetime. Fortunately, it is never too late with God.

If you want to prepare yourself for the next great move of God, then this book will answer most of your concerns, and generate in you a great hunger and love for more of Him which is His Holy Spirit's promise to you. Hopefully it will restore a deep first love passion for Jesus Christ your Saviour, Lord and soon returning King. Many today are like the Ephesian church in *(Rev. 2:4)* and have departed from their first love. A good starting point is to admit that you need much more of God in your life.

Happily the Spirit of God is looming over the entire earth right now, ready to move in unprecedented ways that I believe will eclipse the book of Acts and all of what happened in the early church. Imagine millions of Christians freshly filled and empowered by the Holy Spirit, ready to carry out the mandate of Jesus to His Apostles in *Matt. 10: 7 & 8*. *"As you go, preach this message: 'The kingdom of heaven is near.'Heal the sick, raise the dead, cleanse those who have leprosy, drive out demons. Freely you have received, freely give. (NIV)"*

We need to be as prepared as we can be, not holding back through fears, misunderstandings or even cherished traditions. Our world needs a powerful Christian revival, and we need it NOW!

This book is crammed full of faith building chapters one after another, having to do with receiving the Holy Spirit. Then resting in the love of God, healing both physical and emotional by the Spirit's power. And then how to nurture and continue on in the Presence and Power of the Holy Spirit while at the same time guarding your own resources so that you don't burn yourself out along the way.

Finally, there is a warning for those of us who were fully engaged and part of this or other previous revivals: Don't make the mistake of thinking that you got it all back then. Melinda points out that typically the previous revival resists and downplays or even opposes the next move of God. May none of us make that tragic mistake as we realize that God continues to save the best wine until now. *(John 2:10 NIV)*

We are all admonished, indeed required by the Lord to be activated powerfully by the Holy Spirit to do our part in bringing in the kingdom of God. *"May Your Kingdom come, may Your will be done, on earth, In your city, as it is in heaven!"*

Jesus made it very clear in John 20;21-22, "So Jesus said to them again, "Peace to you! As the Father has sent Me, I also send you."And when He had said this, He breathed on them, and said to them, "Receive the Holy Spirit." (NKJV)

So, as you read this book, receive the Holy Spirit's fresh in filling and be a part of what God does next!

John Arnott

Founding Pastor,

Catch The Fire, Toronto

FOREWORD

By Dr. R.T. Kendall

2021

I first met Melinda Fish in Toronto. I was there in 1996 for the second anniversary of the "Toronto blessing" as it was originally nicknamed by the London Sunday Telegraph. I felt honored to be there then and am still honored to be a friend of John Arnott, the pastor of the Toronto Airport Vineyard Church (later renamed Toronto Airport Christian Fellowship) when the unusual movement of God first broke out in 1994. My first memory of Melinda is that she made me laugh. She was – and is – so funny. I laughed when I heard her speak publicly; I laughed more when I talked with her privately. Her sense of humor is evident in her book which now brings the original edition up to date. But make no mistake; this is a serious book about a serious subject.

The original edition of THE RIVER IS HERE was endorsed by my beloved friend and mentor Dr. J. I. Packer, arguably the greatest theologian in the world, now in Heaven. He was a supervisor of my thesis at Oxford many years ago. I was surprised but pleased that he endorsed this book. Surprised? Yes. Jim Packer was a very cautious man-so cautious that he refused to endorse one of my own books! But when he wrote as he did regarding Melinda Fish's book The River is Here, I knew he would be severely criticized by many of his reformed brethren. Dr. Packer recognized that the Toronto Blessing was not a fad that would pass. He knew that it was of God – even though there were odd and strange things that accompanied it. After all, no great public manifestation of the Holy Spirit is neat and tidy.

I taught for many years that the Charismatic Movement was like "Ishmael," because as Abraham sincerely believed that his son Ishmael was the promised son that God had in mind (Genesis 15:4), Abraham got it wrong (Gen.17:18-19); so too the Charismatic Movement is not the final move of God many looked for but that the best is yet to come. Isaac is coming. That said, it was prophesied that Isaac would be an "ugly baby"; he will "burp like Ishmael, need diapers changed like Ishmael" and would put many people off from believing that something genuine has been born. I have therefore asked, Could Toronto be baby Isaac? I don't know. But as an ugly child can grow up to be a handsome person, could it be that the Word and Spirit will finally come together – and that Toronto was actually the embryonic phase of the next great move of God? I don't know. Who knows? I have to say if am transparently honest, that Toronto and its aftermath have sometimes been more Spirit than Word, as Melinda Fish describes in this book.

When the Toronto Blessing spread to London – manifesting in Holy Trinity Church, Brompton, I was disquieted. I said it was not of God. For one thing, I did not want it to be of God. I found it disgusting. Furthermore, if it were truly of God, it would have come to Westminster Chapel first! The truth is, I was jealous. Ken Costa, churchwarden of HTB, asked to talk to me about this phenomenon. I was prepared to sort him out. But as he talked – not remotely trying to convince me of anything, I began to see in my heart that I was on the wrong side of the issue. A sense of the fear of God came on me; I felt I was in a tradition that had always been against great moves of the Spirit – beginning with the New England Great Awakening (1735-50) up to the Welsh Revival (1904-05). I repented and went to my pulpit and publicly climbed down from my adamant stand – and never looked back.

A famous story comes out of the life of Oliver Cromwell. When someone showed him his portrait that was done by an artist, he noticed that his face was smooth and without any wrinkles or blemishes. He rejected the portrait and instructed the artist to paint him "warts and all". Melinda's book on the Toronto

Blessing shows warts and all! It is my belief, that, if the Toronto Blessing was not the embryonic phase of the next great move of God, it will in any case go down in history as one of the historic moves of the Holy Spirit – not unlike, for example, the Welsh Revival. The Welsh Revival, too, was severely criticized at the time by respected church leaders, although one of the harshest critics, according Dr. Martyn Lloyd-Jones, was struck with blindness as a judgment of God. If you look for things to criticize, you will find them in the Great Awakening, the Welsh Revival and the Toronto Blessing movement.

I recommend Melinda Fish's book to be read far and wide. Read it with an open mind. If you have been a critic of this phenomenon, it could be you are in for the surprise of your life.

If you want to prepare yourself for the next great move of God, then this book will answer most of your concerns, and generate in you a great hunger and love for more of Him which is His Holy Spirit's promise to you. Hopefully it will restore a deep first love passion for Jesus Christ your Saviour, Lord and soon returning King.

R. T. Kendall, 2021

WHY A NEW EDITION?-Melinda Fish

When the late J.I.Packer, the evangelical theologian, read the first edition of this book in 1997, he wrote, "Melinda Fish's gentle book explores the current Toronto-type blessing from the inside. Seeing it not as a fireworks display for sensation-seekers but as an answer for the drooping and discouraged. She gives the best apologia yet for a phenomenon that is now too big to ignore."

I am glad that he saw the intent of my heart in writing this book. Writing THE RIVER IS HERE was the most satisfying writing experience of my life. It is a tribute to the Lord's faithfulness to give us more of Himself fulfilling to us His prophetic word which He gave us in 1976. He promised us a River and gave us Isaiah 43: 18-22 as confirmation. For 18 years we waited. In 1994 the River came.

This new edition examines the revival which broke out in 1994 in Toronto, Canada. It follows the testimonies and the experiences of people who witnessed it firsthand. Although it contains passages lifted from the original book, it digs deeper than the original. The perspective we now have is clearer. The impact of it has traveled to the ends of the earth.

The following is the most accurate description I can give of the events surrounding the lives of people I know who witnessed a Divine intervention in the period beginning in 1994. Far from being dry historical fact, it is drenched with the soppy footprints of the Holy Spirit who chose this way to renew us. May it inspire you to hunger for Jesus Christ and experience the love of God, your Heavenly Father. The Lord Himself inspired the metaphor of "the River" to describe His work. God acts and human beings respond. I pray that your response is holy. This is how we responded.

"...And I know that whatsoever God doeth shall be forever. There is nothing to add to it and nothing to take from it; and God has so worked that men should fear Him...".

(ECCLESIASTES 3:14 KJV)

CONTENTS

1 - THIRSTY

On November 24, 1994, about 6:30 P.M., Ron Dick started the engine of his '91 Mercury Sable and began the 35-minute drive to his church, the Toronto Airport Vineyard, that he had made three nights a week for months. As the freeway from his home in Oakville, Ontario, stretched out before him, he did not know that his faithfulness to his post on the prayer team was about to put him on a collision course with a hungry pastor and family who were especially desperate for a touch from God.

For nearly twenty years, that pastor and his wife had been waiting for revival that had been promised them by nearly every guest speaker who had stood in the pulpit of their church in southwestern Pennsylvania. By this time, the hills and valleys of hope and subsequent disappointment had left them so skeptical that they little expected the power of God to move in their lives in any meaningful way.

From the States, where it was Thanksgiving evening, several hundred American citizens had crossed the Canadian border to spend the holiday in Toronto. The service was not unlike the hundreds of services that had taken place six nights a week since January 20, 1994, when the Holy Spirit had fallen on a sparse crowd. On that January night, Randy Clark, a Vineyard pastor from St. Louis, had been invited by John and Carol Arnott, the pastors of the Airport Vineyard, to begin a series of meetings in the church that met in a strip of businesses on Dixie Drive in Mississauga, Ontario, a few hundred yards from the airport runway. Randy, unsure that he had enough messages to complete the short series of meetings, had brought two staff members with him, hoping they could fill in when he ran out of sermons.

But Randy did not run out of sermons. The power of the Holy Spirit fell that night in an unusual way. Members of the church began to laugh, cry, shake and fall to the carpet under the influence of the Holy Spirit. This happened the next night, too, and the next.

News of the unusual phenomena spread quickly throughout churches in surrounding Ontario. Within days, pastors were attending to see if God was truly there. News also spread through the secular press in Britain. Soon both curious and spiritually dry believers from all over the world were booking flights to Toronto. Two airlines, AirCanada and British Airways, had to add extra flights from London to accommodate the widening flow of seekers.

Word of the outbreak of something unusual reached the ears of those in the United States who read about it in a handful of periodicals, both secular and Christian. Many believers heard about the unusual phenomena through negative reports from a nationally syndicated radio broadcast. So many seekers made their way to the Airport Vineyard in1994 that TORONTO LIFE MAGAZINE named the church Toronto's number-one tourist venue for that year.

On this November night, as an eager congregation crowded into the lobby of the Asian Trade Center in Toronto (later to become the permanent home of the burgeoning fellowship), a local Vineyard pastor, the son of a Baptist minister, began his message with a prayer: "Come, Holy Spirit!" Then he opened his Bible to Numbers 11 and began to speak about Moses, the seventy elders and Eldad and Medad who hadn't come to the meeting that Moses had called. Instead, they prophesied back in the camp where they were, as the Holy Spirit fell on them.

In many ways, Ron Dick, the driver of the Mercury Sable and a member of Toronto's prayer team, was like Eldad or Medad— an ordinary guy. Retiring early after an accident had crushed his back, Ron wanted his later years to count for Jesus Christ.

Years before he had asked the Lord to allow him to be "in on the next move of God." Earlier in 1994, Ron and his wife, Nancy had heard about the moving of the Holy Spirit at the Toronto Airport Vineyard and joined one of the church's home groups. Soon he volunteered for the prayer team, hoping the Lord would use him to spread the blessing to others.

After a period of worship, as the evening message began, one side of the congregation in the 2500-seat auditorium began to erupt in a wave of laughter. After the message ended, people were asked to stack their chairs and line up in rows for prayer. They did, and hundreds of people stood waiting for something.

Then prayer team members began to make their way through the crowd. Ron Dick sought those who looked ready to receive prayer and began to lay hands gently on each one. The power of God began to overcome one after another in the crowd, as it had for months. Soon the majority of the nearly two thousand people present were lying on the floor. Some were laughing while others were crying out, shaking or weeping. Others lay quietly as though engaged in prayer. A few stood transfixed like oak trees by a river, soaking quietly in the Lord's presence.

After a few minutes, Ron stopped in front of the middle-aged couple—the pastor and his wife from Pennsylvania. He touched the wife on her forehead so lightly that she could hardly feel it. But a few seconds later she, too, was lying on the carpet, swept off her feet for the first time in her life by the power of the Holy Spirit.

When she and her husband returned to the States four days later, the renewal they had expected for more than two decades finally broke out in their church.

I will always be grateful to Ron Dick and all the people at that church because my husband, Bill, and I were the couple.

Where We Came From

It had taken the Lord several months to break through our skepticism. Like other pastors, we had grown weary of expecting and not seeing. The Body of Christ in the United States had gone through a particularly dark period that began in the late 1980s. In spite of a continuous trickle of salvations, the Charismatic Movement that had made the '70's a glorious decade in modern Church history had waned and the receding wave had exposed the debris—-scandals created by the impure motives of those who tried to capitalize on God's power. Church attendance fell off nationally. Boredom put churchgoers to sleep as frustrated pastors resorted to seminars and programs to motivate believers to faithfulness.

Bill and I were no exception. In 1976 we moved from Dallas to Pittsburgh to the the pastorate of a small, inner-city congregation. Before we left Texas, Bill had an actual vision. He saw a mighty river of water forming as the snow on a mountaintop melted. The force of the water built up behind a dam on the mountainside, forming a large crack. At first a large teardrop of water oozed through the crack, but soon the force of the water burst the dam, and the mighty river flowed down the mountainside. In the next scene, Bill saw the river begin to trickle out the front doors of a small, weather-beaten church building in the middle of a desert. As the water began to flow, the river became deeper and wider until it covered the desert. Finally, on the banks of the river, signs of life began to appear.

After our arrival in Pittsburgh, a pastor from Dallas we knew came to visit and felt God impressing him with a Scripture passage for us that included these verses:

"Do not call to mind the former things, or ponder things of the past. Behold, I will do something new, now it will spring forth: will you not be aware of it? I will even make a roadway in the wilderness, rivers in the desert...I have given waters in the wilderness and rivers in the desert, to give drink to My chosen people." Isaiah 43:18-20

A few months later, in a bookstore that was closing, Bill found a copy of Arthur Wallis' classic on revival, IN THE DAY OF THY POWER. As he flipped through it, one passage caught his attention. On page 47 was a description of the same vision Bill had seen before leaving Dallas.

"In picture language," Wallis wrote, "this is revival."

But he went on, "Often in the period just preceding the movement, the stream of power and blessing has been unusually low. The people of God and the work of God have been in great affliction and reproach, despised or ignored by those around them."

This is the desert.

In one of my previous books, RESTORING THE WOUNDED WOMAN (Chosen, 1993), I described the emotional upheaval Christians often face when their heartfelt desires and prayers go unanswered. In the wake of repeated disappointment and deferred hope, the heartsick Christian often lapses into depression and despair. The result is what I call the "barrenness syndrome."

The barrenness syndrome is characterized by an inability to bear natural or spiritual fruit. It is also characterized by shame, since prayers and faithfulness seem to remain unrewarded. Christians with the barrenness syndrome, weighed down by a constant sense of shame before others, may also feel victimized by God through experiencing the common reverses of life. They may become angry with Him and withdraw from fellowship, since they have had their hopes revived and crushed repeatedly and are afraid to stir up hope even one more time.

Causes of the barrenness syndrome are as numerous as the individuals who suffer with it. Each personal dream that goes unfulfilled, each hope or prayer shattered by situations beyond the believer's control, may lie at the root. Fruitlessness is one of the most severe tests of a Christian's life—one that all of us face about something.

For many believers, the past several years had brought a sense of barrenness. Between 1976 and 1994, Bill and I became all too familiar with it. We held out hope and faced disappointment when every year for nearly twenty years failed to bring the hoped for revival. Although the congregation in Pittsburgh had been established, it remained small. We had arrived with hope and faith, but after nearly two decades, we faced the possibility that revival might not come to pass, that we had been somehow mistaken or that we had been driven only by naive enthusiasm.

Our pastoral staff met often to discuss what we would do if we could not find enough volunteers to staff the Sunday school classes. We usually lacked enough money to pay the salaries. We were accustomed to smallness and the fact that the baptistry had not been filled with water in years. Growth was limited to dissatisfied believers migrating to our congregation from other congregations. We derived our sense of self worth as a congregation from mission trips devoted to ministries of helps for missionaries on the field. But when we considered the lack, we were overwhelmed by our sense of powerlessness and the shortage of resources available to accomplish the task.

Bill and I seemed caught in a cycle of discouragement with the congregation. When we were up they were down, and when they were up, we were down. In 1993 we spent long periods in soul-searching. It was the lowest point in my Christian life. In 1994 I endured major surgery, followed by hormone shock and began to experience panic attacks. The future, I feared, would resemble the past—and that thought brought waves of discouragement and fear.

Bill and I determined that we could wait no longer. We had let our dream die of seeing God's blessing on our congregation, and so we sent resumes out of state in the hopes that the Lord would take this as His cue to open another door. We had lost our vision.

People in this condition cannot pray with expectancy for revival. Something must happen to revive their spirits so that they can believe. Hunger for God must be reignited by the Lord Himself.

But when we arrived in Toronto, accompanied by our fifteen-year old son, Bill, we realized to our amazement that we were not alone in our despair. Thousands of pastors from Tasmania to Finland, from Korea to South Africa, had also lost their visions or faced trials equally devastating. They were coming to Ontario in the hopes that God would revive them.

But does any Scripture passage indicate that God confines Himself to manifesting His presence in one location more than another?

Why Toronto?

In I Samuel 19 King Saul, angry and jealous of David, not only threatened David's life but tried on two occasions to murder him. David fled in fear to the prophet, Samuel, in Raman. But Saul, intent on killing David, sent messengers to where Samuel and his school of prophets were meeting and prophesying. As the messengers entered the area, they too began to prophesy, rendering them incapable of carrying out Saul's orders. This happened to three sets of messengers. Finally Saul decided to get David himself. But as he entered the area, he, too, fell to the ground, stripped off his clothes and began to prophesy "all that day and all that night." (Verse 24).

The powerful presence of God had been manifested at a certain location for a certain purpose.

The church in Toronto has seen seeker and skeptic alike fall under the influence of the Holy Spirit's presence and experience unusual manifestations. Every time God brings revival, there is usually a visible outpouring as happened ninety years ago during the Azusa Street revival in Los Angeles. The Holy Spirit fell on a church in a poor neighborhood mission at 312 Azusa Street. For blocks around, the Lord seemed to have set aside a radius devoted to His presence. Unbelievers who entered that area were drawn inexplicably to the meeting and converted.

But some ask whether it is necessary to go to Toronto, "Can't God move on me where I am?" My answer is this: if you faced the possibility of dying in the middle of a desert and realized that an oasis was not far away, to what lengths would you go to in order to find it?

Why visitation comes in one place and not another is known only to God. Still, it is only natural to wonder why He moves in one place first. Did people there do something special to warrant the blessing?

Supernatural revival falls on people as a work of grace. Like all other works of the Holy Spirit, it is poured out not because people earn it, but because they need it. When John Arnott, pastor of the Toronto congregation, formerly known as the Toronto Airport Christian Fellowship, is asked why the Lord chose his church in Ontario on which to pour out His renewal, he sometimes replies, "Because it's near the airport." Then he confesses freely that he does not know why. The staff and members did not expect to host a "ground-zero" visitation beginning in 1994, nor do they feel they did something to merit the favor of God. Like Mary, the mother of Jesus, they were surprised. They were not hungrier for God or praying more than anyone else. They simply wanted the Lord and had promised not to quench the Holy Spirit if and when He came.

John Arnott points out that in the days before matches existed, there were two ways to start a fire. You could stand there and rub two sticks together, or you could go to your neighbor who already had a fire burning and take a coal back to your fireplace. Bill and I were too weary to rub sticks. When we heard that fire had fallen in Toronto, we decided to go. Cold, tired and hungry, we set out to investigate things we had been told.

This book, then, is about the river of blessing that has sprung up in our day—-a river that has begun to flow in may places throughout the world. Although one fountainhead seems to have been a church in Toronto, this river is actually flowing from the presence of the Heavenly Father. At the end of the day, it will not matter where it started. What matters is that you realize God wants to direct His river through you to the dry places around you. When God's river flows, it is no longer necessary to pray for it, but rather to recognize it and open your life and the doors of your fellowship to the blessing of the Holy Spirit.

But recognizing a real move of the Spirit is not always easy, especially in the beginning. In fact, the river of God's visitation often resembles the way Jesus Christ came the first time. A visitation often has a small beginning in an obscure place like Bethlehem.

This book is about what happens when the Lord visits His Church. The word "visitation" in Greek is derived from the verb "episkeptomai" which means "to inspect, to go to see." In every season of visitation, the Lord goes 'to see' His Church, to look her over. Is she ready for His coming, to be His bride? Is she loving Him?

Examine with me the current renewal sweeping the Church. In it are keys to understanding how God moves in every day of true visitation. What are the earmarks of genuine revival, so that we may not be like the Pharisees of Jesus' day and miss the day of visitation? Is there a scriptural basis for the unusual demonstrations of power? We will explore how a visitation challenges the wineskin of every local church and tests her ability to conform to the new thing God is doing. We will see how great leaders in Church history experienced their own days of visitation and how leaders are responding to the current renewal. How will it affect you and your local congregation?

But above all, how can you recognize your own day of visitation and open your heart to Him?

2 - IS IT THE REAL THING?

One Sunday morning not long before our trip to the Toronto Airport Vineyard, something unusual happened in our church. Linda Bock, the nineteen-year-old daughter of one of our deacons, was singing with the worship team as usual. As the congregation paused between songs, Linda began to laugh and cry at the same time. In the back of the auditorium, her father stood up and (since we are a Charismatic church that believes in the gifts of the Holy Spirit for today) gave a message in tongues.

To my surprise, the interpretation flashed through my own mind immediately like words in the line of a book.

"I want to come into the church and do things you have never seen Me do before, touch people in ways you have never seen Me touch them before and use people you have never seen me use before. All I want to know is, do I have your permission?"

We all clapped and said, "Yes, Lord!"

But about a month later, when Bill and I got back from Toronto, God actually showed up. He was hard to recognize at first, and how He came proved to be nothing like I had expected.

The Effect

After Bill and I returned from the Airport Vineyard, we called all the members of the church together on a Wednesday evening to discuss what was going on in Toronto. Several had already been influenced by the syndicated radio program that was issuing negative, even erroneous reports about the meetings there.

They felt skeptical, to say the least. But as we shared what we had seen, a special sense of God's presence began to hover over our small congregation.

Our son, Bill, testified about his experience in Toronto. He, too, had been on the floor under the power of the Holy Spirit. He amazed everyone by associating this experience with things God had promised our congregation in years past.

"God told us that it's springtime in the Church," Bill said fervently, " and this is it. You sow seeds in the spring. God is sowing seeds for the harvest with what is happening now."

Until that moment, we had no idea our teenage son had been meditating on the prophetic words spoken to our congregation.

One by one, other members of the church began to worship, pray and weep under the sovereign power of the Holy Spirit. It was as though the Lord was once again indicating His intent to come in and do "something new."

The following Wednesday night, my husband called everyone forward who wanted to receive prayer. Bill had experienced no external manifestation himself while we were in Toronto, other than quiet weeping. Now, as he prayed for the members of our congregation, he purposely did not touch them for fear of being accused of pushing them over. Yet as he prayed for them, one after the other began to drop to the floor as if overcome gently by the Lord's unseen hand.

We were amazed not only that they were falling, but at the ones who were falling—those we least expected to succumb to "emotional displays."

The first person to fall down under the influence of the Spirit was Nancy Westerberg, who for ten years had been our faithful children's pastor. She has a quiet, reserved demeanor but had been in a depression for several months. Now her petite frame hit the floor at the same time that her feet began to move up and down as though she were drum-rolling them on the carpet. Her arms began to sway back and forth in the air. This went on for several minutes. Suddenly she jumped up and took my hands and shouted, "Dance with me, Melinda!"

I was startled but I did not know what else to do. Nancy and I twirled around the front of the sanctuary.

Nancy told us later that she had been experiencing depression, but that it immediately lifted. For nights afterward, even in her sleep, she would feel her feet beginning to dance. Her heart began to dance, too. This was December 1994. The depression has not returned.

Suddenly we understood why the Lord had asked our permission to move in His own way. He was, He said, going to touch people as He had not done before. The blessing would come with some humbling manifestations. We had a choice to make: Were we willing to pay the price of being thought of as strange, or would we stop these emotional outbreaks and risk quenching the Holy Spirit?

The River

For years Bill and I had held onto the Scripture passage that our minister friend from Dallas had given us at the outset of our ministry in Pittsburgh: "I will do something new, now it will spring forth...I will even make a roadway in the wilderness, rivers in the desert..." (Isaiah 43:19). But I never considered the fact that throughout Scripture, rivers are places of testing.

The Jordan was a testing place for Naaman the Syrian before it was a place of blessing (see 2 Kings 5). The commander of the Syrian army had become infected with leprosy. The soldiers in the army had heard that a prophet in Israel could heal. Namaan's dilemma would be comparable to the North Korean dictator having to come to Pittsburgh for a heart transplant. When Elisha sent Naaman to the Jordan to dip seven times, the commander was angry. Happily for him, his servants persuaded him to humble himself. He was healed on the seventh dip.

In another situation, when Gideon's army was being chosen for battle against the Midianites, the Lord told him to take the men to the river (see Judges 7). The method each man used to drink the water determined whether or not they were selected for the battle.

It is no coincidence that the metaphor for the current visitation of God is the river. Although the waters of a river are refreshing and life-giving, they bring fear to the hearts of many. As their course deepens and becomes more forceful, those who are afraid of rising water head for dry ground.

Every revival in Church history has been accompanied by unusual signs which some refer to as manifestations of the power of God. There is no such thing as a revival without "mess." The messy aspects of revival are usually the characteristics that draw attention to it and signal a change in the seasons of God. The "mess" is an affront to tradition, which has been established in part by what happened during the previous move of God. If weeping and repentance were earmarks of the previous revival, then those acquainted with that movement tend to expect tearful repentance in the next move of God. But what if God changes gears? What if the familiar earmarks are not prominent? This has the unsettling effect of making the revival unrecognizable to those who are unable to change.

To have been an active part of one move of God, therefore, does not ensure that you will be part of the next. Church history is full of examples. As we will examine in a later chapter, some of the followers of Martin Luther drowned Anabaptists; Anglicans persecuted Methodists; mainline denominations opposed the Assemblies of God; then they opposed the Latter Rain movement. Be sure that many who were involved in the Charismatic renewal will oppose what comes next.

But these days we are to be humble rather than critical. When the flood of God comes, it destroys man made objects in its way —but we may not know which objects are man made until the River hits them. Jesus cautioned all of us to build our houses on the rock, because wind, rain and floods may break out against them and cause them to fall. Interestingly, each of these metaphors—wind, rain and floods—is commonly used to describe revival, a move of the Holy Spirit. All these natural phenomena, as well as a river raging out of its banks, are beyond the control of human beings.

Something New

For years I quoted the phrase "something new" with the revival I prayed for, while I assumed subconsciously that what would happen would repeat what happened in previous revivals with which I was familiar.

My own idea was birthed in Baptist tradition. To us revival was not real unless people engaged in open confession of sin, repentance with tears, and public salvation or rededication of their lives to the Lord. Revival usually occurred in scheduled meetings that lasted for a few days. Often we would go to the altar, weep, feel the effects for a while, then return to business as usual at church. No alterations were ever made in our church program, other than yearly changes in calendar events and volunteer personnel. It never occurred to us that we should expect God to move in any other way.

Then, in the early 1970s, while Bill was in seminary, we saw a visitation of the Lord that brought spiritual renewal to Beverly Hills Baptist Church in Dallas, TX. People could sense the presence of the Lord even in the empty auditorium. Before services the crowd overflowed out the doors and into the lobby. More than once, unbelievers who did not intend to go to church were drawn in off the sidewalk as they passed by the building. Sometimes people were at the altar under conviction of sin and committing their lives to Christ even before the choir came in to begin the service.

To witness the impact of that visitation was powerful. I still remember decades later, the awesome sense of God's presence that enveloped us all and equipped us for service. Supplementing the memory of revival meetings from my childhood, now I framed this experience in my mind as true revival: weeping, repentance, people being touched by the Holy Spirit, the irresistible grace of God, perhaps a few miraculous healings to kick everything off and attract the lost. If a visitation by God was real revival, I assumed, the church would fill quickly with new believers.

Letting go of this as the only model for real revival is difficult. I imagined myself during the coming revival (whenever it came) as ready to be used to lead others into a relationship with Jesus. After all, I had known Him for decades, had been filled with the Holy Spirit more than twenty years before, and had endured the dry season faithfully. Besides, I had read many books about revival and was certain that when it broke out, I would recognize and embrace it quickly.

But I was not prepared at all for what happened. In fact, initially I rejected it because it was not what I expected.

The first thing I had heard was that "holy laughter" had broken out in a church that our friends, Dick and Barbara Olsen, attended in Wilmington, North Carolina, and in another church in Chichester, England. Jane Campbell, my editor, told me about laughter breaking out in other areas of the body of Christ. These friends broached the subject cautiously, knowing that Bill and I did I not go in for fads.

Why, I wondered, would God do something like that? Laughter was naturally contagious, too easy to mimic. Besides, laughter seemed out of place in a world with so much sorrow, a world that needed the Gospel so desperately.

Nor did Bill and I place any value on falling in response to prayer. We had seen many people fall from the power of suggestion or be given a shove by an overeager evangelist. Too many, in our opinion, were like the guards who came to the Garden of Gethsemane to take Jesus away. They fell under the power of Jesus' presence but got up and arrested Him anyway. Falling did not seem to have a prominent place in Scripture, and we did not see enough fruit from it to seek such an experience ourselves.

These were the reasons we always gave for resisting "emotional experiences"—in this case, holy laughter and falling under the power of the Spirit. But deeply embedded in our minds was a rigidly defined framework for what revival and church life should be like. This framework was created more by our previous experience than by Scripture. And it suggests how tradition is formed: by doing things the way we always have, without considering change.

Tradition is also formed by what never happens. Because we may never have seen something—-a miracle, for example—we cannot believe it, so we feel compelled to develop a theology based on why there are no such things as miracles. Or we get used to "doing church" in the context of our particular denomination and assume that, at least for us, it will always be that way. So then if God wants to get to us, He must work within the box we have drawn for Him.

But when revival comes, God does not necessarily accommodate our traditions that interfere with His purposes for the moment. He begins to take His divine crayons and color outside the lines. When God says He will do something new, why do we assume it will be something we have seen before? We seem to think He will surprise only unbelievers. Unfortunately, many sincere believers, even those who have been seeking the Lord for revival for years, often miss the day.

Why Do We Miss The Day Of Visitation?

One day Jesus wept over Jerusalem, the promised city full of religious people:

> If you had known in this day, even you, the things which make for peace! But now they have been hidden from your eyes....They will not leave in you one stone upon another, because you did not recognize the time of your visitation.
>
> (Luke 19: 42,44)

Is it possible to be in God's presence and not know it? Won't I be able to recognize the real power of the Holy Spirit? But the Pharisees of Jesus' day could not or would not, even though they knew the Scriptures thoroughly.

There are several reasons we can miss a move of God.

Resistance To Change

Soon after renewal broke out in our church, I attended a motivational seminar sponsored by the realtors from several local offices in our franchise. The speaker showed a video on the subject of human reaction to change, which pointed out that the initial natural response of human beings to any form of change is usually negative. The video offered as examples scientific breakthroughs made by obscure people working every day at their jobs. Because these people were "common" workers and were not perceived as innovators, their inventions and discoveries were rejected at first at the executive levels of their companies. In fact, the workers, rather than being praised and promoted, were actually shown the door.

One example of resistance to change took place when the seat of the watchmaking industry was still Switzerland. A workman in a Swiss factory discovered that a quartz crystal, cut in a certain way, could be vibrated at a certain frequency and made to run a watch. But the executives of his company were unable to see the value in such a discovery and discarded it. Whoever heard of a watch you do not have to wind? It took the Japanese to buy the idea of a quartz watch and revolutionize the watchmaking industry.

Tradition has the power to hold back blessing when it blocks our vision and prevents us from making the necessary paradigm shift so we can implement change. In the same way, revival tests the theology and flexibility of the Church to recognize and yield to the power fo the Holy Spirit.

Preconceived Ideas Of Revival

I have already shared that I nearly missed this current blessing because what was happening did not fit my idea of what a revival should be like.

A few months after renewal commenced in our congregation, I traveled to Arizona to speak in a church there. After the meetings, I was with some pastors in a restaurant when they ran into another pastor who had returned recently from Toronto.

This clergyman, who had been involved in the Latter Rain revival in the 1940s-1950s (a revival characterized by healings and miracles and recognition of the five-fold ministry as described in Ephesians), had attended two or three evening services at the church in Toronto. He offered the following assessment to us in the restaurant: "They don't know what they're doing up there. It's nothing we haven't seen before. And anyhow, they won't be able to hold onto it. I handled it by writing a report and handing it out to my congregation."

His attitude reminded me of the ten spies who came out of Canaan with a negative report. All I could think in response to his assessment was, for God so loved the world, that He did not send a report.

I could not resist sharing with this pastor my own reactions to the current move of God. My testimony, I hoped, would inspire him to take a second look.

"Our experience was completely different," I told him and the other ministers as the table. "For my husband and me, the power of the Holy Spirit has been life-giving and refreshing and has brought the beginning of a long-awaited season of blessing. When we returned to our church, we decided to open the doors to it. And the Lord has actually revived our congregation through it."

But he did not seem open or even interested. I realized then that except for the Lord's mercy to me, I would have had the same attitude.

In order to recognize the Lord's presence when He comes to visit, we must be willing to give up preconceived notions about revival that are shaped by experiences of the past. Remember that passage from Isaiah: "Do not call to mind the former things, or ponder things of the past." (Isaiah 43:18)

The pastor in the restaurant could not open his heart because his idea of revival was limited to the way God moved in the Latter Rain revival. To him, revival only meant healing, prophesying, salvation and baptism in the Holy Spirit. He wanted to hear the old songs and see God act in precisely the same manner to the younger generation.

Christians from a non-charismatic or non-Pentecostal background look for revival differently. But the assessment of any of these may be similar to that of the people of Jesus' day: "Can anything good come out of Toronto?"

Misapplied Scriptures

Sometimes we flee to the Scriptures - or our interpretation of Scriptures - for refuge from the rising water. The Pharisees tried this, too. But with their hardened hearts, they overlooked certain prophetic passages. They did not expect the Messiah to come from a poor family. They expected a warrior who would judge like the Gideons and Joshuas of the past. So through what glasses are we reading Scripture? I have been amazed to sift through every experience common to this renewal through Scripture and find evidence in its pages. (We will look at this evidence in chapter 4.)

In Christian tradition, certain myths arise like proverbs and come to govern our analysis of whether or not a movement is from God. How we love to quote Paul's letter to the Corinthians, "Let all things be done decently and in order." But is our idea of "decently and in order" how the Lord sees it?

We say, for example, "The Holy Spirit never interrupts Himself." Kathryn Kuhlman used to say this whenever an over-eager person would try to draw attention to himself by delivering a prophecy or a message in tongues in her meetings. While it was right for her to do this, what she said became a rule throughout the Charismatic Movement. However, the Holy Spirit interrupted Peter's message to Cornelius' friends with a demonstration of power: "While Peter was still speaking these words..."(Acts 10:44)

Another "proverb" we quote is, "If something is from God, you won't be afraid." But almost every time an angel appeared to anyone in Scripture, the person was terrified and the angel had to reassure him with "Fear not..."

We also say, "If it's God, you'll be able to understand it because God doesn't create confusion." But when Jesus ascended into heaven, He left the disciples scratching their heads about many things that He had said. He had even told them, "I have many more things to say to you, but you cannot bear them now. But when He, the Spirit of truth, comes..." (John 16:12-13)

I have read numerous articles decrying the fact that what is happening now is not really a revival. Real revival is supposed to look another way, and we should not play this up bigger than it is. It is as if they are saying, "This may be God, but I don't believe I need it. I'll wait for something more powerful, something closer to my definition, to come along."

Who are we to diminish anything God is doing? Can't God do something new in His Church? Perhaps He is accomplishing His ends with unusual means. Perhaps He is again doing something as non-traditional as His healing the man born blind (see John 9). He spit on dirt and anointed the man's eyes with "mud" to enable him to see, offending Jewish tradition on the Sabbath. The end was worth the means to everyone but the Pharisees.

Honest Skepticism

Another reason we may miss a move of God is honest skepticism. Luke praised the Bereans for being "more noble-minded than those in Thessalonika" (Acts 17:11) because they examined the Scriptures daily in response to Paul's message, to see if these things were so. Healthy skepticism is born of a sincere heart that truly wants God and is willing to search out the truth and acknowledge if God is there. No one wants to fall into error through gullibility.

How is it possible, then, to discern whether a move is of God before you commit to it? Sometimes you will not know until you jump into the River and experience it for yourself.

In the early days of the Charismatic Renewal, Dr. Howard Ervin, then a pastor from New Jersey, had similar advice for John Sherrill who was at that time a non-Christian reporter analyzing the spiritual phenomenon of tongues. Dr. Ervin compared John's dilemma with a trip to a little Gothic chapel with a red door which he stopped by the road to admire.

"My eyes would try to follow the soaring lines of the building upward as Gothic architecture makes you do, but every time they were jerked back to that red door. It was so flamboyant, it kept me from seeing the whole picture."

"Tongues, John, are like that door. As long as you stand outside, your attention is going to be riveted there and you're not going to be able to see anything else." Once you go through, however, you are surrounded by the thousand wonders of light and sound and form that the architect intended. You look around and that door isn't even red on the inside. It's there. It's to be used. But it's has taken its proper place in the design of the whole church.

"That's what I'd hope for you, John. I think it's time for you to walk through that door. If you really want to discover what the Pentecostal experience is all about, don't concentrate on tongues but step through the door and meet the Holy Spirit." (They Speak with Other Tongues, Chosen, 1985), pp.114-115.

To step through the door, to jump into the River, takes courage. And being willing to acknowledge later that we have been mistaken is humbling indeed.

Bill and I went to Toronto because an Episcopal priest and his wife that we know, George and Joanne Stockhowe, encouraged us to do it. They had attended services there for a week and written a favorable newsletter to thirty of their friends. They took time to point out certain Scripture texts and mention things that were said from the pulpit of the Airport Fellowship. One point that caught my attention: Joanne's observation that "there were no 'stars' at that church, no glittering personalities, only nameless people who were refreshed by what God seemed to be doing there."

So we decided to investigate. Like the shepherds who were told of Jesus' birth on the hillside near Bethlehem, we said to ourselves, "Let us go to Bethlehem [or in this case, Toronto] and see this thing which has come to pass." I fully believed that if it was a real visitation of the Lord, He would let me know.

By the time we arrived there, I sensed that unless I was touched by the Lord soon in a refreshing way, I would never be able to fulfill His plan for my life. I was, I realized, "wretched and miserable and poor and blind and naked." (Rev. 3:17)

At the Wednesday morning ministers' session, Dr. Guy Chevreau, a Baptist minister from Ontario, was speaking about the historical significance of the unusual manifestations that had accompanied this outbreak of the Holy Spirit's power. Like any pastor, I needed to hear that these manifestations were biblical and had happened to others in Church history. I was relieved to learn that throughout Church history, there had been numerous manifestations of laughing, fainting, crying out, jerking or "quaking" and other noisy activities in response to outbreaks of God's power. I was surprised to learn that John Wesley, the founder of Methodism, and his brother, Charles, the great hymn writer, were both overcome by holy laughter for more than an hour while walking through a field one day. The experience caused them to be full of the joy of the Lord's presence.

During the Great Awakening, similar manifestations occurred to the believers in the area of Northampton, Massachusetts, in 1735. Jonathan Edwards wrote in an essay entitled, " A Narrative of Surprising Conversions," (Edwards on Revival, Banner of Truth Trust, 1994):

> "It was very wonderful to see how persons' affections were sometimes moved—when God did as it were suddenly open their eyes, and let into their minds a sense of the greatness of His grace, the fullness of Christ, and his readiness to save—after having been broken with apprehensions of divine wrath, and sunk into an abyss under a sense of guilt which they were ready to think was beyond the mercy of God. Their joyful surprise has caused their hearts as it were to leap, so that they have been ready to break forth into laughter, tears often at the same time issuing like a flood, and intermingling a loud weeping." (p. 37)

As Guy Chevreau finished his talk, I knew that what was going on in this church could not possibly be all wrong as some had reported. Nor could it be all the flesh, as others had surmised.

Throughout that first trip there, I scrutinized everything to make sure it was Christ-centered. If it was a true work of the Hoy Spirit, I knew it would draw attention to Jesus Christ. Some eager reporters had so focused on the unusual manifestations that I had not been able to see how Jesus Christ was being honored. But as Bill and I listened to testimonies from the platform of those who had been touched in the renewal, we noticed one common thread: Christians who had been apathetic churchgoers like us had been transformed into lovers of Jesus Christ through the means of receiving prayer at every service from other believers. Those praying for others were people like Ron Dick (who I mentioned in chapter 1)—-not big name speakers, but ordinary people who had themselves been touched by the Lord.

One woman's testimony called to my heart. She and her husband had been chronic TV-watchers and had all but quit going to church. When one of her friends phoned to tell her God was moving at the Airport Vineyard, they went out of curiosity and received prayer. She wept as she testified how precious Jesus had become to her. While she talked, she "jerked" every few seconds. But I didn't notice that as much as I noticed how much she loved Jesus now, whereas before she had no emotion for Him. It was her testimony that made me want to receive prayer again, because I was not only curious; I was hungry. And when you are hungry, you can hardly resist going to see for yourself. I was so moved by her testimony that I became willing for God to touch me, even if He needed to crack my proud resistance, regardless of what He needed to do.

Let's take a closer look at the River itself. What kind of blessing is it bringing?

3 - WHAT DOES IT MEAN?

As the Lord began to bring us a new sense of His presence and power, we faced the same questions that confronted the onlookers on the day of Pentecost. In their amazement and perplexity, they cried out, "Whatever could this mean?" (Acts 2:12, NKJV) It is the same response of the Israelites to the manna God sent from heaven to feed them in the wilderness. In fact, the very word *'manna'* means "What is it?"

Asking what something means is a natural reaction as our human understanding searches for a way to process the workings of a God who has suddenly broken out of our control and invaded our "normal" lives with something unexplainable.

Since the renewal with its accompanying signs has spread to churches all over the world, we can recognize certain earmarks of what has become known as the "Toronto Blessing." But first let's look at the blessing itself.

What Is The Blessing?

The "blessing" is a refreshing wave of the Holy Spirit that is empowering congregations with a renewed sense of the heavenly Father's love and power. It was named the "Toronto Blessing" by the British press who saw the outpouring at Holy Trinity, Brompton (HTB), an Anglican Church in London's Knightsbridge section, across the street from the famous Harrod's department store.

In May 1994, Ellie Mumford, wife of John Mumford, pastor of

the South London Vineyard church, made a brief holiday visit to the Toronto church. She had heard of the unusual manifestations that for four months had accompanied the refreshing wave of God's power as the news spread through the world wide Vineyard Fellowship grapevine. Feeling dry spiritually and in need of a season of refreshing, she attended the services and received what has become known as "soaking prayer"-repeated or extended prayer. Ellie Mumford was overcome by the "blessing" and refilled with the Holy Spirit and a divine expectancy that this was the beginning of a new move of the Holy Spirit.

On her return to London, she shared her experiences with her friends on the staff of HTB. In a meeting, as she began recounting her experiences, the Holy Spirit fell on the members of the staff. Each one fell to the floor overcome by a sense of the presence of the Lord. They also began to laugh uncontrollably. After several hours, the church secretary thought she had better phone the minister in charge.

Sandy Millar, who was the vicar of HTB, was attending a meeting of the Evangelical Alliance elsewhere in London. He was summoned from that meeting to an "urgent" phone call.

"I just thought you should know," the secretary told him. "The entire staff of the church has been slain in the Spirit and is lying on the carpet. They are all laughing."

Not wanting to let on to his evangelical colleagues who were within earshot, Sandy whispered into the phone, "Is that a good thing?"

" It's a wonderful thing!"

"Well, if it's so wonderful, what are you doing on the phone?"

"I crawled," she replied.

The following Sunday morning and evening services, Ellie Mumford shared her testimony with the congregation of Holy Trinity, Brompton, about receiving the "blessing" in Toronto. The same signs and wonders accompanying the Toronto Blessing began to occur that very day among the parishioners of HTB.

Throughout the summer of 1994, queues of people lined up

outside the church before every service attracted the attention of Fleet Street, the seat of the British press. It had been a long time since the people had to line up and get assigned tickets for available seats for any event in Britain besides a rock concert. And for church? Out of curiosity journalists began to attend services. Every newspaper tabloid carried stories of the outbreak of revival. The press soon dubbed the unusual phenomenon "the Toronto Blessing."

Before the outpouring at HTB, similar signs and wonders had occurred randomly in several other places in Britain, but HTB, perhaps because of its influence in London, became a center of the renewal that affected thousands of Anglican parishes and other churches in England. The revival in Sunderland, for example, became one of Britain's centers of renewal holding services six nights a week. It traces its renewal to the day the pastor of the Assembly of God church there, Ken Gott, went to HTB and was touched by the power of the Holy Spirit.

The influence of the renewal broadened beyond the scope of the Vineyard fellowships and into the mainstream of spiritual life in England. To date more than six thousand churches there from various denominations have been renewed by the "blessing". Many attribute the spreading fire to a unity among churches in Great Britain—a unity that has yet to exist in America. The renewal in Britain is now at revival proportions and is accompanied by the beginnings of an increase in healings and an ingathering of the lost.

What is happening in the U.K. should give us faith for America- a prophetic portent of things to come if we open our arms to the new blessing God is pouring out.

Earmarks Of The Blessing

Since the renewal, with its accompanying signs, has broken out in churches all over the world, we can recognize earmarks of what has become known as the Toronto Blessing.

"Carriers"

The wave of the Holy Spirit's power in this renewal is bringing to the thirsty a long-awaited drink of living water. Those who have been affected throughout the world have begun to unify around a renewed awareness of the Heavenly Father's personal touch on their lives and a deeper intimacy with the Lord Jesus Christ. But although the blessing seems to be falling on some congregations sovereignly, the majority have been touched by someone who can trace the blessing back to receiving prayer with someone who had been similarly touched in Toronto, or the evangelistic meetings of Rodney Howard-Browne, a South African evangelist.

The blessing is transmitted through yielded vessels by the laying on of hands in prayer. The person who transfers the blessing is usually one who is usually open to receiving more of the Lord's presence in his or her life. Many of those who seemingly transmit the blessing, however, are "carriers" who have never experienced any outward manifestation themselves.

The term "carrier" may have originated with Stuart Bell, leader of Alive, Lincoln (formerly known as New Life, Lincoln, England). Stuart leads the Ground Level team, a stream of churches in Britain. Stuart traces his experience to the day Dr. R.T. Kendall, pastor of Westminster Chapel in London, the renowned evangelical pulpit, came to his church to speak.

Dr. Kendall appeared to be delighted to be invited to speak in a charismatic church and urged Stuart, at the close of the day of meetings, to open the altar for prayer. He encouraged the Lincoln church to be free to close the meetings as they saw fit. He had heard of renewal and had received prayer himself, although nothing external had happened.

Later, over dinner, Dr. Kendall expressed his dismay at not receiving any outward sign.

Stuart, responding with concern, heard himself blurt out, "Well, we ought not to rely on our feelings..." Stuart went on nervously, "...perhaps you are a 'carrier' of the blessing?"

Later, before he left, Dr. Kendall prayed for those gathered in

Stuart's office. Then he said, "If anything unusual happens to any of you within the next 24 hours, let me know."

The next day Stuart was scheduled to speak at two churches. The first was Ichthus, whose pastor was Roger Forster. The church had been holding meetings for a week already; people were being blessed and touched by the Holy Spirit's power. Stuart relates what happened next:

> Suddenly there was a sense that the spiritual climate in the room was rising. Roger asked me to pray for him. About halfway through my prayer, I was taken totally by surprise as Roger and I were knocked to the floor for about twenty minutes. I personally felt the power and love of God like "warm waves" passing over me. There were manifestations of laughter, tears, confession of sin, humility, brokenness. For five hours there was the very evident blessing of God upon our lives...

Stuart went on to speak that evening at the Baptist church in Newark, UK. At the end, the leaders asked Stuart to pay for them. Again, the power of God fell, moving the leaders to laughter. The result: a deep work of the Holy Spirit in their lives.

Stuart notified Dr. Kendall immediately by mail of the extraordinary events that had occurred within 24 hours of the prayer with him in Stuart's office. To which Dr. Kendall replied: "Wow!"

The "spreadable" quality of this outpouring is an earmark of real revival. It does not belong to one denomination or fellowship, but to the body of Christ.

Ordinary People

Nor is the renewal centered around any personality. While many have been newly filled with the Holy Spirit at the evangelistic meetings of Rodney Howard-Browne, the South African evangelist, the renewal is not limited to meetings where he is present. In fact, a new day has dawned on the Body of Christ.

On the day of Pentecost, the Lord fulfilled Moses' prophecy in Numbers 11:29: "Would that all the Lord's people were prophets, that the Lord would put His Spirit upon them!" On Pentecost the Father made the Holy Spirit available to everyone who would trust Jesus as Savior and Lord. Throughout the centuries, history has recorded isolated instances of blessing beyond salvation for the hungry and thirsty, but not until the Azusa Street revival in Los Angeles in 1906-1909 did the Holy Spirit begin to be poured out corporately with signs and wonders, similar to those on Pentecost. *How do we know? Just because it isn't recorded doesn't mean it didn't happen.*

Throughout fresh waves of revival in this century, we have seen a gradual increase in the outpouring of the Holy Spirit, accompanied by speaking in tongues, prophecy and the other "sign" gifts of I Corinthians 12. The Charismatic Renewal—which started in 1959 with Dennis Bennett and other Episcopalians in California, and which multiplied in 1967 with an outpouring on a Catholic prayer retreat at Duquesne University in Pittsburgh—spread the Pentecostal blessing throughout hungry churches in mainline denominations. Since then new denominations and unaffiliated churches have sprung up as a direct result of this outpouring.

During the charismatic renewal, an experience subsequent to conversion known as the baptism in the Holy Spirit spread through the prayer of not only clergy but ordinary people touched by the Spirit's power. It was the dawning of a day in which we realized that the Holy Spirit is no respecter of persons, but He will use any surrendered believer to transmit His blessings.

The Toronto Airport Christian Fellowship (now called Catch the Fire), because it was organized in the Vineyard model established by John Wimber had already trained prayer teams to minister to those who answered the altar call in their services. So when the Holy Spirit fell on January 20, 1994, the ministry of the prayer team became vital to the spreading of the blessing. As hungry seekers began to attend the meetings, prayer teams of ordinary Christians (with extraordinary commitments to the Lord) found themselves ministering literally to the world.

The prayer ministry of ordinary people and the practice of rotating speakers at the Toronto meetings, using local pastors to fill the pulpit, gave a nameless, faceless quality to the renewal.

These practices de-emphasize the need for one revivalist to pray for those seeking prayer and make it possible for the anointing to be distributed through regular folks willing to allow God to use them. Perhaps these wise decisions are two of the factors that have perpetuated renewal in Toronto and encouraged the worldwide spread of the blessing to the literal ends of the earth.

They have also encouraged another aspect that sets this renewal apart from others.

"Soaking" Prayer

Instead of receiving the entire benefit of the current renewal in one experience, those affected most deeply testify that the Holy Spirit's presence within them and the work He does through them grow stronger as a result of receiving repeated prayer.

During this renewal, the blessing is spreading in churches and home prayer groups through the practice of "soaking prayer." "Soaking prayer" is a phrase that came to life in the Charismatic Renewal, primarily through the ministry of a renewed Catholic priest, Fr. Francis McNutt. He applied the term for those who needed to receive the prayer of attentive believers over an extended period of time. The term is not found in Scripture, but the concept is. It is a prayer of "waiting" or "resting" in God's presence, allowing Him to minister to you.

The church in Toronto began to notice early in the outpouring that those who surrender to prayer repeatedly begin to experience an increasingly powerful touch in their lives. It is as though the ground is saturated through repeated waterings of the Holy Spirit as though "out of their innermost beings begin to flow rivers of living water." It is a way of "seeking" the Lord expecting the Holy Spirit to keep them constantly filled with the Holy Spirit to "all the fullness of God."

Because so many have seen visions about life-giving water, the metaphor of the revival quickly became the "River." It is as though the seekers have found God's presence like a river flowing through a desert. As they submerge themselves continually, they become aware that the Lord Jesus becomes more precious to them, their passion for Him is renewed. In the same way that a river restores a dry landscape into a lush field, the river of renewal has been refreshing the parched lives of God's people. Their desire to share Him with others has begun to flow, and they are constantly thirsty for more of Him.

Visions And Dreams

One of the unusual aspects of this visitation is that those under the influence of the Holy Spirit actually see visions—mental illustrations—similar to the people in times when the Scriptures were recorded. Some people today have seen pictures of the deep workings of the Holy Spirit to heal their bruised emotions. Young men and women in our own congregation have received visions of the Heavenly Father demonstrating His affection for them. Others have seen visions concerning the coming harvest, the deepening river and the awakening of the Church.

The Charismatic Renewal of the 1960s and '70s saw an increase of such prophetic activity, but the prophetic dimension poured out on believers of all ages and from many countries and walks of life has seen a dramatic increase. In fact, visions have become so common that their frequency is almost taken for granted. The power of the Holy Spirit that accompanies the visions, bringing release from bondage and a sense of divine expectation, testifies to the fruit of them.

In October 1994, the month before Bill and I visited Toronto, we made a two-week trip to England and stayed with our friends Kevin and Pam Swadling. They, like other friends, told us of the River that washed through their fellowship. We remained adamant that such a fad meandering through the Church would soon die out and expose the fact that the "revival" had been a counterfeit.

During the Sunday morning service at their church, Chichester Christian Fellowship, the congregation prayed for us. One of the members of the congregation, although she knew nothing about us said during that prayer time, "You have been waiting on God for years. Everything you have been waiting on God for is just behind a curtain, and He is about to part the curtain." We did not know then that we were in the same fellowship where Arthur Wallis, author of IN THE DAY OF THY POWER, was the pastor before his death!

I did not doubt that this message was from God, but I was in such a state of dryness that I was tired or hearing prophecies. I wanted a day of fulfillment.

That evening a contingent of people from that church who had just returned from the Airport Fellowship in Toronto gave their testimonies. Still skeptical, Bill and I allowed them to pray for us. Nothing happened. At least, nothing we noticed then.

A week later we were in Madrid visiting our friends, Mary and Elliott Tepper. I dreamed one night that I was in a restaurant with Bill, when I spotted at the next table a healing evangelist and his wife. I went over to their table and began to pour out my heart, telling them how badly we needed to see revival.

Suddenly the countenances of the couple changed and became that of two men. One of the men interrupted me and said, "Have I not promised you times of refreshing from the Lord?"

When those words left his mouth, they became alive inside of me. I do not know how else to say it. And in the dream, I felt myself overcome by the Holy Spirit's presence as though I had been "slain the Spirit"—although I had never had that experience in my life.

The next morning I awoke with a profound awareness of the presence of God that I had not felt in years. All that day and the next, I had the sense of His presence, and the beginnings of a revival of hope in my heart. I did not realize it, but the River was beginning to lap at my feet. I was beginning to thirst for more of the Lord's presence and became willing to do anything to be filled by Him again.

Within a few days, I began to "see" clear pictures in my mind describing the Lord's intentions for this renewal in my own life, in the life of our congregation and in the Body of Christ.

Joel prophesied:

And it will come about after this that I will pour My Spirit on all mankind; and your sons and your daughters will prophesy, your old men will dream dreams, your young men will see visions. And even on the male and female servants I will pour out My Spirit in those days. (Joel 2:28-29)

A few weeks after the renewal began in our congregation, while we were praying, I saw in my mind's eye, the Lord Jesus standing chest deep in a river. People were standing on the bank gingerly sticking their toes into the water. As they did so, the Lord would grab them one-by-one by the ankles and yank them into the river. He exclaimed, "I've been looking forward to the day of visitation more than you have!"

Seeing the Lord's great pleasure concerning the renewal gave me a sense of rest. Having struggled with the deep-seated fear of abandonment, I have often subconsciously projected that fear of abandonment onto my Heavenly Father. I have been anxious concerning His willingness to revive the Church and to bless me with this outpouring. I have also experienced a false pressure to "earn" the blessing. This one picture provided a giant step in my emotional healing and a great encouragement to others struggling with the Lord's willingness to bless them.

This gracious understanding of the Lord's overwhelming desire to bless and revive the Church affects two other aspects of this outpouring.

Intercessory Prayer

The disappointed hearts of many Christians have quenched their desire to pray. When faith is at a low ebb, it is difficult to pray with expectation. I have already said that Christians in that condition cannot pray for revival— at least not with expectation. Repeated cycles of hope and disappointment affect the believers' view of God and cause them to be suspicious of God's desire to answer their prayers positively. But one of the wonderful aspects of being constantly filled with the Holy Spirit and the deeper sense of intimacy with God that accompanies it, is that it transforms one's view of the Lord into a more accurate one. What if you knew that the Lord to whom you were praying was like the Lord chest-deep in the the river, laughing and saying, "I've been looking forward do this day of visitation more than you have?" Would that impart more faith and expectation to you to believe that He would answer? Rather than shouting at Him as though He was so far away that He couldn't hear you or transforming your posture in prayer to one of pleading as though you needed to draw His attention away from matters more important,—what if you could simply speak to Him knowing that His love for you and desire to bless you are constant...That's why Jesus said, "If you then being evil know how to give good gifts to your children, why wouldn't He give the Holy Spirit to the one who asks?"

Knowing God like this causes you to want to pray, to be alone with Him, to worship Him in Spirit and in truth because it blesses Him.

Wouldn't the Father have more delight in our prayer meetings if we were like joyful, expectant children just wanting to be with Him? Wouldn't you rather come home to a family of kids who were happy and joyful and sincerely glad to see you than to a bunch of whining, manipulative kids who were acting like orphans expecting the worst from you, begging and pleading for something you didn't really want to give?

The more a Christian is filled with the Spirit, the less anxious he is, the more he trusts the real God and His love. The renewed spirit prays from an intimate relationship with God, not from a formal, distant and fearful one.

The work of the Holy Spirit renewed our ability to pray. Instead of asking Him to do what we desire, we ask Him what He wants us to pray for. As the group waits on Him, a thread of concern emerges. The people experience His desires in the form of mental pictures, auditory impressions and even passages of Scripture that He applies to the situation, imparting the will of God in a particular matter. Praying with the spirit, not with the understanding, is transformed into a language of intimacy rather than a "clanging cymbal." Isn't this a better way to pray, "making intercession for the saints according to the will of God?"

One Friday night in our congregation, our regular intercessory prayer meeting in a room next to the sanctuary coincided with a wedding rehearsal going on in the sanctuary. As we waited on the Lord, asking Him what to pray for, several minutes elapsed. Two women independently of one another received a "picture" from the Lord with the idea that He wanted us to pray for people to be healed in the congregation. As we began to pray about this vision, the Lord began to fill our mouths with laughter. For several minutes we laughed in what we knew was victory.

Later we learned that several people in the wedding party wanted to abandon the rehearsal and come into the prayer meeting—a far cry from the days when no one wanted to intercede because it seemed like such an intense and fruitless pursuit, full of vague purpose and morose appeals to God for things we didn't think He wanted to answer anyway.

Praying in the Holy Spirit has another amazing effect on a believer's life that we are seeing around the world, a love for the Scriptures.

Love For The Scriptures

If anyone needs proof that the Bible is the divinely inspired word of God, look no further than this earmark of revival. Not only does the Holy Spirit move God's people to pray but He also increases their desire to read and meditate on the Scriptures. Believers who a year ago were hard-pressed to read bits of Scripture in a printed daily devotional guide, are beginning to linger over the Bible, finding it full of personal, intimate messages.

One of the first manifestations I noticed after several years of dutiful reading only to get a sermon, I was surprised that my affection for the word of God had returned. The thought of reading it excited me.

After the Great Awakening, Jonathan Edwards wrote,

While God was so remarkably present amongst us by His Spirit, there was no book so delightful as the Bible...Some, by reason of their love to God's word, at times have been wonderfully delighted and affected at the sight of a Bible...A Narrative of Surprising Conversions, p. 47

Revival seems to have that effect on everyone, regardless of the era in which they live. But there are other remarkable aspects of the Toronto Blessing.

Physical Manifestations

As in other revivals in past centuries and in the recent past, the invasion of God's power has brought about unusual phenomena in the form of physical manifestation. Because accounts of these phenomena have often been edited out of modern versions of early revival literature, the Christian today is left with the impression that revival invaded the Church in past times unobtrusively. But this is not true.

The phenomena that accompany today's outpouring are similar in nature but much more widespread, reaching worldwide proportions. They are responsible (as in the past) not only for drawing attention to the new thing God is doing but also for engendering criticism and providing a stumbling block to those who want a "clean" revival.

Let's look at them now.

4 - WHY CAN'T WE HAVE REVIVAL WITHOUT THOSE MANIFESTATIONS?

Two days after Bill and I returned from Toronto, I became angry perhaps because all I had seen was so new. I did not understand why God would make all those people laugh—including me. So I began to reevaluate everything, thinking perhaps I had been caught up in the emotion of the moment. *Why can't we just have revival without all those crazy manifestations?* I wondered.

"If this is really God," I told my husband, "why wouldn't He move on someone in our church and make them apologize for some of the pain they have caused us in the last twenty years?"

I was still looking for a sweeping move of repentance that always accompanies revival.

Two hours later, the doorbell rang. Standing at our back door was Jennie Blackham.

Jennie and her husband, Paul, had met in our church. Bill had performed their wedding ceremony ten years before. But the time had been difficult for them. Although they both have college degrees, Paul had been unable to find a job since financial problems had forced him to leave Bible college. Jennie had suffered two miscarriages, and the weight of so much unresolved emotional pain had driven them to the brink of despair.

We watched them sink under the weight without knowing how to do anything except pray for them and accept them problems and all.

Finally, Paul and Jennie decided they needed another church setting. Bill and I did not try to stand in their way. We have found it best through the years to bless people as they go. But Jennie felt she had much in her heart that she needed to express.

After they left the church, I received a long letter from Jennie. It came on day that was already a low point for me. I was struggling with my own emotional pain. The words of the letter stung. I managed to pull myself together, and Bill and I sent them a card and invited them back anytime they wanted to visit.

Now here she was at the back door. But in place of the dark expression we had become accustomed to, her face was glowing. She was holding a peace offering—a wool suit, my colors.

In shock I invited her in. She wanted to talk to me about what had happened to her.

After they had left our congregation, Jennie said, they had begun visiting another church whose pastor had been to Toronto. During an altar call, she had gone forward for prayer. When the pastor touched her forehead, she had fallen to the carpet and laughed hysterically for 45 minutes as the Lord pulled out of her a deep plug of emotional pain.

Jennie did not have to tell me she was different. In place of despair, I saw hope. In a few moments the Lord had been able to touch her in a way that hundreds of our sermons and teachings had not.

Jennie visited awhile and left. I cried for several hours. It was as though Jesus had been so close to me that He had listened in on my angry outburst earlier. He had heard it as a prayer and answered it immediately.

What is God doing?

God Invading Our Boundaries

I used to believe that God would not do anything in a church service to make me feel uncomfortable. I wanted to hear the "rushing, mighty wind" as long as it did not mess up my hair! Emotional displays have always unnerved me—unless, of course, they were coming from me. I know how far I will let myself go, but I do not know how far other people will go. But sometimes God offends us to show us attitudes that are in His way. I have heard that the late John Wimber, founder of the Vineyard Fellowship of churches, would often say, "God will offend your mind to reveal what's in your heart."

But why do we feel uncomfortable?

Civilized human beings have a fear of shaming ourselves. To behave outside the bounds of propriety, to violate the rules, may bring about disapproval from others and result in rejection. Many of those rules have been instilled in us by our parents who wanted us to know how to behave socially so that we might be accepted, and, for heaven's sake, not embarrass them! As adults we eschew circumstances where things may happen that embarrass us or make us feel ashamed.

But that sense of shame becomes false when we feel ashamed over what God is doing. Let the Lord expose your false sense of shame and replace it with a willingness to be humble enough to allow Him room to move, even though the emotional responses of others to His power may embarrass you a little. Believe me, the fruit is worth it. And you will come to love God better when He is out of *your* control!

The preaching of John Wesley apparently created surprisingly emotional responses among his listeners. From his journal of June 15, 1739 we read this:

> Many of those that heard began to call upon God with strong cries and tears. Some sunk down, and there remained no strength in them; others exceedingly trembled and quaked: some were torn with a kind of convulsive motion in every part of their bodies and that often so violently that four or five persons could not hold one of them...I immediately prayed that God would not suffer those who were weak to be offended. But one woman was offended greatly being sure they might help it if they would; no

one should persuade her to the contrary; and was got three or four yards, when she also dropped down in as violent an agony as the rest.

(*THE WORKS OF JOHN WESLEY,* Baker, 1991, p. 204)

But let's examine the ministry of Jesus to see if he was sensitive to what others might think about what He said and did.

The Embarrassing Jesus

Not long into the ministry of the Lord Jesus, the disciples realized that to follow Him meant that they had to bear with the unusual and unexpected. In fact, Peter wrote in his epistle that "to you who believe, He is precious; but to those who are disobedient...'a stone of stumbling and a rock of offense.'" (I Peter 2:7-8, NKJV)

Jesus did not seem to care what anyone thought when He talked with a Samaritan woman at the well; nor what the host of a banquet he gave in Jesus' honor when He received the worship of an adulterous woman who invaded the formal affair; nor what the Gerasenes thought when Jesus commanded the legion of demons to go into the herd of pigs; nor what religious people thought about His failure to observe Jewish traditions that had risen up around the Law of Moses, such as eating with unwashed hands. He cared more about the needy than about how human beings interpreted and defined the Sabbath.

Jesus purposely said things He knew would offend. "Unless you eat the flesh of the son of Man and drink His blood," He declared in the synagogue, "you have no life in yourselves."(John 6:53) He did not bother to explain it; He just let it fall. Multitudes were so offended that they stopped following Him. On another day Jesus cried out at one of the most solemn moments of a Temple ceremony in front of a huge crowd, "If any man is thirsty, let him come to Me and drink..." (John 7:37) On at least two occasions, He wept in front of others.

I do not know if you want me to continue. There are plenty more examples. But in all these things, Jesus was testing the love and loyalty of hearers and followers alike. He was invading man-made boundaries of religiosity and propriety that stood in God's way.

I am not giving permission to the overzealous believer to interrupt services without concern for the authority of the local church. I *am* asking Christians to take a long, hard look at their own traditions and whatever makes them feel uncomfortable. Ask yourself this question before you rule out renewal or any particular manifestation: *What if it is God?*

When a person demonstrates emotion, that emotion origin-ates in one of two places: the soul or the spirit. Sometimes it is not so easy to discern the origin in another person by simple evaluation based on one's comfort level. Ask the person what is taking place in her heart. If a manifestation is truly Christ-centered, you will see evidence of His ministry to them: a new freedom, a sense of His presence a godly desire being restored, a healing that glorifies Him.

Before we look at the manifestations themselves, let's look at some scriptural evidence for reasons God uses signs and won-ders.

Why Signs And Wonders?

Whenever God begins a new season, He usually gives us a ser-ies of signs. If we are watching for Him, we will see these as sig-nals that the old day is passing and a new day in God is dawning.

Just before Jesus was born, the Lord broke a four-hundred year prophetic silence in Israel by sending an angel to Zacharias, the father of John the Baptist. The angelic visitation frightened him. But Gabriel tried to put Zacharias' fears to rest and give him a message he had waited for personally and ministerially all his life. He and his barren wife, Elizabeth, would have a child who would be the prophet to usher in the long-awaited Messiah. Zacharias was so surprised and frightened that he did not fully believe it.

We may want to criticize Zacharias for his unbelief, but could you accept something today unquestioningly that had not happened to anyone since the 1500s or even since Bible times? By Zacharias' day, religious people had adopted (as some have today) an erroneous doctrine -that miracles had ceased and that God only did that as the Scriptures were being written. It is a doctrine based on experience or the *lack* of experience, in this case.

The message of the angel Gabriel was the first in a series of visitations to ordinary people. Apparently there was no one God wanted to use as a prophet. Or perhaps, at this most special moment in human history, the Lord simply preferred to send an angel. In any case, these supernatural occurrences signaled a break between the Old and New Covenants, the day of the Messiah's coming to Israel.

The ministry of Jesus was full of signs and wonders—-statements He made that fulfilled prophecy and miraculous occurrences that drew attention to the fact that He was more than a prophet; He was the Son of God.

After Jesus died on the cross, rose from the dead and ascended into heaven, He sent the Holy Spirit to mediate God's activity on earth. But the Holy Spirit did not "sneak up" on human beings without warning. Another wave of signs and wonders signaled His coming.

On the Day of Pentecost, the Holy Spirit fell on the waiting 120 believers with the sound of a forceful wind that filled not only the room where they were sitting but the entire house. (Acts 2)

The advent of the third person of the Trinity falling on the disciples in power caused manifestations that made other people wonder. Flames of fire hovered over the believers' heads and they began to speak in languages they had not learned—-something that had never happened in human history. Then when Peter preached his famous message on the Day of Pentecost, enabled by the Holy Spirit to speak to people from other places and cultures, they *heard* the gospel of Jesus Christ in their own tongue. Several thousand were added to the Church within the next few days.

Later this sign happened to others receiving the Holy Spirit (see Acts 10, 11, 19) We know that tongues were given to the Apostle Paul and many other Christians, because Paul instructed them on the proper use of praying with the spirit as opposed to praying with the mind, and on the public manifestation of tongues with interpretation in a meeting (I Corinthians 14). Paul wanted the manifestations of the Holy Spirit's power to bring glory to Jesus Christ. In those early days of the Church, "everyone kept feeling a sense of awe; and many wonders and signs were taking place through the apostles."(Acts 2:43)

Signs and wonders do produce awe, and apparently, in this case, they were too numerous to mention. But what possible glory can God receive from of the manifestations in this twentieth-century (1994+) renewal?

At first this question plagued me. But our ways are not God's ways. Sometimes, in the Church, we who know Jesus lose our awe of Him. Faith ebbs and we revert to "maintenance mode." But the lost are seldom attracted to a church that is in maintenance mode.

So what must God do in order to refresh and renew those who have accepted Jesus and have been walking in the Spirit? What if God's people have been disillusioned with the miraculous and have lost faith in His willingness to do the impossible? Although some might say He should not do anything, God is full of mercy and is love. He knows our weak frames and longs to wash our feet again with a refreshing sense of His presence.

That is one of the chief purposes of revival: to renew the saints in their faith. God must get the attention of Christians who are used to business as usual at church. Is it possible that He would choose to invade our lives with a new wave of the power of the Holy Spirit and use different signs and wonders that cause us to investigate, question and be in awe of His sovereign majesty and the ability to "bowl" us over?

Signs and wonders born of the Holy Spirit always glorify Jesus in some way. Jesus Himself warned of other "great signs and wonders" that will draw attention to false prophets who will "mislead if possible, even the elect" (Matthew 24:24). Signs and wonders alone, then do not signify the work of the Holy Spirit. Remember the signs performed by the magicians in Pharaoh's court alongside those performed by Moses and Aaron? If, on the other hand, we see a church being infused with a hunger for God and deep love for Jesus Christ, we may assume that God Himself is somewhere behind the manifestations.

Jonathan Edwards faced the same challenges during the Great Awakening in 1735 that we face today. He wrote, "There was never any great manifestation that God made of Himself to the world without many difficulties attending it." ("Distinguishing Marks of the Work of the Spirit of God," *Edwards on Revival, p. 133*). During Edwards' meetings, many were overcome by "tears, trembling, groans, loud outcries, agonies of body, or the failing of bodily strength." Edwards also observed that the presence of these manifestations did not indicate whether the work was from God or not from God. Rather, he detailed numerous ways to discern the presence of the Holy Spirit in the wake of such things. One of the chief evidences to Edwards was love:

> Therefore, when the spirit that is at work amongst the people... brings many of them to high and exalting thoughts of the Divine Being, and his glorious perfections; and works in them an admiring, delightful sense of the excellency of Jesus Christ; representing him as the chief among ten thousand, and altogether lovely, and makes Him precious to the soul; winning and drawing the heart with those motives and incitements to love...the wonderful free love of God in giving His only-begotten Son to die for us, and the wonderful dying love of Christ to us who had no love to Him but were his enemies...it must needs be the Spirit of God...

Physical Manifestations

What, then, are some of the phenomena taking place in the current outpouring of the Holy Spirit. Is there biblical and historical precedent?

Groaning Too Deep For Words

On my first trip to Toronto, at the end of the service on the first night, I could only sit and watch during the prayer time. Hundreds of people lay on their backs on the floor. Some were crying out, others were laughing, some were shouting, even roaring. I did not now what to make of it. My main experiences were both Southern Baptist and relatively calm Charismatic ones, the only outward manifestation in the congregation was sitting in the pew and facing forward from which we conducted services in the usual manner. It took me 24 hours to get accustomed to the atmosphere without allowing the goings on to distract me from the reason I came: seeking a fresh touch from Jesus. I could not understand why such a large group of people, most of them pastors, would be affected like this.

Once I began to receive prayer myself, however, the Lord recalled a scripture to my memory:

...We ourselves, having the first fruits of the Spirit, even we ourselves groan within ourselves, waiting eagerly for our adoption as sons, the redemption of our body...And in the same way, the spirit also helps our weakness; for we do not know how to pray as we should, but the Spirit Himself intercedes for us with groanings too deep for words. (Romans 8: 23, 26)

Although we think we have a "framework" for groaning in intercessory prayer—a wordless prayer that cannot be articulated—suppose there is more to it? Suppose the infinite God invades a human spirit with such a vast display of love and power that the person can only cry out?

Some believers find themselves groaning as a woman giving birth. Sometimes such groaning is associated with intercession or with the "birthing" of a message from God, a vision or a ministry.

Examining the fruit (as Jonathan Edwards recommended) will help those of us who are used to seeing such gut-wrenching manifestations only when demons are being cast out. Early in the renewal, in fact, we were certain that most of us on the floor were crying out because they were receiving deliverance.

Indeed, some of these may be receiving a sovereign releasing touch from the Lord. When Bill and I questioned most of them later, however, we discovered that the joy of God's presence was so overwhelming that they could only cry out in joy. Others were seeing visions with coordinating sounds.

Groaning may take many different forms. One of the most unusual to date is roaring -- a phenomenon John Wesley encountered. From his journal entry for April 17, 1739:

> Soon after, two other persons (well known in this place, as laboring to live in all good conscience towards all men) were seized with strong pain, and constrained to "roar" for the disquietness of their heart. But it was not long before they likewise burst forth into praise to God their Saviour.

A woman named Sue (1994) from our congregation was always a friendly, joyful person, always affirming and full of love. One day as she was receiving prayer lying on the carpet near the altar, she sensed a roar welling up within her. Gentle, friendly Sue began to roar so loudly that we were startled.

During the next service she testified that while she was on the floor, the Holy Spirit showed her some serious situations involving people in her life she had to confront. She is not, by nature, a confronter. In fact, she tends to avoid confrontation at all costs. But the Lord was showing Sue that He would give her the authority and power to do so. And at that moment, she began to roar. Since then the Lord has given her unprecedented boldness to speak to co-workers and friends about Jesus, as well as to prophesy. But she is not alone.

During one of our special renewal weekends, Stuart Bell, pastor of what is now Alive, Lincoln, and a leader in the "new" church movement in Britain, preached a message from Amos 1:2: "The Lord roars from Zion..." His point was that the lion roars whenever injustice prevails in the land.

During a meeting in England, while Stuart was receiving prayer and soaking in the Lord's presence, he realized two teenagers were roaring over him. Later he heard them crying out in deep agony of soul, "The poor, the poor, the poor..." Earlier the Lord had been interceding through them with groanings too deep for words, and now was giving words to accompany their profound burden. Indeed the lives of these two young men do bear out an increased concern for the poor.

As we examine the Scriptures, we see that many of the prophets accompanied and reinforced their prophetic themes with prophetic acts. Moses, Isaiah, Jeremiah, Ezekiel, Hosea and others all acted out their prophecies. Moses struck the rock, Isaiah went naked and barefoot for three years. Jeremiah bought a field. Ezekiel lay on his side for a full year. Hosea, under the instruction of the Lord (don't try this at home!) married a prostitute. Amos wrote, "A lion has roared! Who will not fear? The Lord God has spoken! Who can but prophesy?" (3:8)

From months of observation, I have come to believe that a new prophetic anointing is coming to enable the Church to function in greater authority. I am seeing an impartation of divine courage to the faint hearted to proclaim the Gospel.

If God has chosen the weak and foolish things to confound the wise (see I Corinthians 1:27, KJV), there will be times He uses our mouths and causes us to break out of our inhibitions. Some church auditoriums may literally be turned into prophetic schools full of Christians being acted upon so powerfully that they go forth courageously to speak in love anything God wants them to say that will draw the lost into a loving relationship with their Heavenly Father.

Laughter

A year ago our daughter, Sarah, was afraid to speak to anyone about salvation. Last summer while home from college, Sarah began to receive prayer at the altar at every service and she became filled with the Holy Spirit, the love of God and concern for the soul of a young man who worked across the hall from her in her summer job at the mall. One day she walked to the mall and spent two hours talking to him about the unfailing love of Jesus Christ, the joy she had found and his need to accept Jesus as Lord and Saviour. The young man surrendered his heart to Christ that evening.

The manifestation Sarah had been experiencing the most frequently was "holy laughter."

The first time I heard this manifestation, I was convinced that those giving themselves over to it were attempting to stir themselves up. I have no doubt that this *is* happening to some. There is evidence in Scripture, however, for laughter on the part of God and on the parts of people being acted upon by God.

The psalmist sang,

When the Lord brought back the captive ones of Zion, we were like those who dream. Then our mouth was filled with laughter and our tongue with joyful shouting...Those who sow in tears shall reap with joyful shouting. (Psalm 126:1-2, 5)

Holy laughter is a release of great joy over the saving and delivering work of God. It follows a long period of captivity and represents a sign of victory. The righteous laugh at the evil man in Psalm 52:6 for that reason. And before the Lord judges his enemies, He laughs at them in Psalm 2:4 and 37:12-13. The writer of Ecclesiastes says there is "a time to weep, and a time to laugh." (3:4) Jesus promised those who weep now that "you shall laugh" (Luke 6:21)

When Abraham was promised by God that within a year his son would be born, Abraham fell to the ground and laughed. Sarah also laughed in her tent and lied to the angel about having done so. When Isaac was born, Sarah said, "God has made me laugh, so that all who hear will laugh with me." (Genesis 21:6 NKJV) When God removed the curse of barrenness from Abraham and Sarah and fulfilled His promises to them, He put laughter in their mouths as well as in their arms. The name *Isaac* means "laughter."

The entrance of God's only begotten Son into the barren life of the oppressed should cause laughter and rejoicing, too.

Today we are seeing God once again putting laughter into the mouths of those who were once oppressed and freeing them from depression and grief. Allowing the manifestation (as others as well) seems to strengthen the sense of God's presence and to quench it seems to diminish it.

Linda, a schoolteacher with a master's degree and gentle demeanor, served our congregation faithfully for over 15 years as the church secretary and administrative assistant. She never did anything to draw attention to herself. She served the Lord contentedly in the background. One night she was sitting on the church pew near the front watching while others receive prayer. Suddenly, she fell over onto the pew convulsing with laughter. She laughed for more than an hour when finally, her husband helped her to their car. We only hoped that she would not be arrested for disturbing the peace! Forty-five minutes later, Linda, still overcome with paroxysms of laughter called on the phone. I put the phone on speaker because Linda was laughing and trying to say something. We could not help laughing, too, as the whole situation was humorous to us, too.

Finally, Linda managed to say why she had called. When she arrived home, she happened to look at her calendar and happened to notice the date. It was on this same date five years ago that her younger sister had died after suffering terribly with cancer. Through gasps between laughs, Linda managed to say on the phone that the Lord had told her He was lifting her burden of grief and that she would never grieve that loss again.

The Lord had also directed Linda to the story of the Prodigal Son. She had worried for five years about her sister's eternal destiny. Linda had not known whether she had ever truly received Jesus Christ as her Lord and Saviour. In all of the happy chaos, Linda's eyes had fallen on a scripture on her open Bible on the desk, "For this my son was dead and is alive again; he was lost and is found." (Luke 15:24, NKJV) It was God's way of letting her know that her sister was home, safe in the arms of her Heavenly Father.

The Lord broke Linda's yoke of heaviness and grief by putting laughter in her mouth as a sign and wonder that a new day was dawning—a day of deliverance from the overwhelming sadness that had weighed down her heart.

In 2021, Linda writes, "God continues to show up in my life in many other tangible and intangible ways, confirming over and over His presence, love, mercy, healing, revelation kindness, correction, protection, direction and power. What stands out loud and clear for me since 1995 is that my Father in heaven "knows my name, address and telephone number, not to mention the number of hairs on my head. Renewal moved that concept from my brain to my heart, right from the beginning. Thank you, Jesus, that I will never be the same!"

In previous revivals, God put laughter in the mouths of many of those whom He filled with the Holy Spirit. Jonathan Edwards and John Wesley were both overcome with holy laughter. In his book **REVIVAL** (Whitaker House, 1983) Winkie Pratney quotes a newspaper account of the Welsh revival meetings with Evan Roberts:

> It may be observed that the dominant note of the revival was prayer and praise. Another striking fact was the joyous and radiant happiness of the evangelist. It's has been remarked that the very essence of Roberts' campaign was mirth. To the rank and file of church ministers, this was his most incomprehensible quality. They had always regarded religion as something iron-bound, severe, even terrible. Evan Roberts smiled when he prayed, laughed when he preached ...(p.175)

Why have we always linked holiness with solemnity? Is it perhaps because of the vision of the great white throne of judgment in Revelation 20? But those who love Jesus' appearing will not shrink from Him in fear. Heaven—where there will be no more tears, sorrow, crying or pain—will be filled with sounds of joy like nothing we have ever heard. As much as any earthly father loves to arrive home from a hard day at work to a home full of joyful, happy children ready to hug him, I believe that the Heavenly Father is putting laughter into our hearts and mouths to relieve us of sorrow and fill us with the Holy Spirit.

I further believe that the laughter we are seeing now is a sign from God that He is about to bring great triumph to the

Church as we gather in the harvest. The laughter seems to have a prophetic as well as healing quality. Proverbs 15:13 (KJV) says, "A merry heart doeth good like a medicine; but a broken spirit drieth up the bones..." In the light of the heaviness and discouragement that have prevailed over the Church recently, could the Lord be filling our mouths with laughter as a sign that new day of miracles, release and joy is dawning?

Convulsive Spasms ("Jerking")

Some believers like the woman I heard testifying my first night in Toronto, or like Haley, a young Englishwoman we will meet in chapter 5–feel their stomach muscles contracting involuntarily, causing them to "jerk." This phenomenon appears in the revival meetings of Edwards, Wesley, Finley and many others, including the multi-denominational Cane Ridge revival of 1801 in Cane Ridge, Kentucky in which 25,000 were converted to Jesus Christ. This event is known as America's Second Great Awakening.

"Drunkenness"

Laughter can become so overwhelming and lengthy that it results in a state akin to drunkenness. There are also people who, when the Holy Spirit falls on them, become "drunken" almost instantly.

On the Day of Pentecost, something similar occurred to the believers on whom the Holy Spirit fell. The observers, drawn to the scene by the tongues and sounds of wind, asked what everyone who hears of the outpouring are asking: "Whatever could this mean?" (Acts 2:12) Other bystanders began to accuse the disciples of being "full of new wine"(verse 13). But Peter, never shy to speak out, set them straight: "These are not drunk, as you suppose..." (verse 15)

Why would onlookers charge that those who had received the Holy Spirit were drunk? Because something was happening visibly to the disciples besides speaking in other tongues. No one is accused of being drunk because he or she is speaking in a

language the onlooker can't understand. It is reasonable to con-
jecture that the fullness of joy accompanying the infilling of
the Holy Spirit produced in them a state resembling inebriation,
perhaps accompanied by laughter or exuberance.

Paul knew about such fullness and advocated the experience
for everyone:

> Be not drunk with wine, wherein is excess; but be filled with the
> Spirit; speaking to yourselves in psalms and hymns and spiritual
> songs, singing and making melody in your heart to the Lord.
> (Ephesians 5:18-19, KJV)

Have you ever seen television programs showing saloons
in the old West? Invariably patrons got so drunk that they
laughed even at things that were not funny, ridiculing their own
problems loudly crowing, shouting, dancing on tables. These
are manifestations of drunkenness. Likewise, there is an overwhelming joy that floods the human soul on being filled with
the Holy Spirit that may also, if intense enough, cause similar
responses! Many of the more unusual vocal responses observed
during this renewal may fall into this category.

Laughter is known to release endorphins into the body that
actually give an individual a pervasive sense of well-being.
Laughter is known to build up the body's ability to fight off
disease. Psychologists have pioneered a new field of study to explore the effects of laughter and other emotional states on the
immune system. No wonder the Scriptures encourage us to take
advantage of this natural medicine for the soul and body!

One of the most unusual and prolonged manifestations happened to a friend of ours, a pastor from England, John Scotland.

The Drunken Man

Many people would love to see signs and wonders, but how
many want to become one? The Old Testament prophets displayed the word of the Lord to Israel in various unusual signs
including lying beside a tile for weeks on end and streaking
through the streets. Had these happened in our day, the prophets

would have doubtless been dubbed insane and arrested.

John Scotland of Liverpool, England was always a Pentecostal preacher with a powerful ministry of the Word that often spilled over into the prophetic dimension. He had been a pastor of a congregation and knew what it was for unusual happenings to occur, but he also knew how to squelch them if things were too out of hand. Little did he know that God was about to overcome him in such a way that he became a sign to all and at great personal expense.

In '94, John was in a meeting where he witnessed a number of people experiencing drunkenness in the Spirit. John found himself wishing he could experience this himself and said to God that he would like to better understand what he was seeing, if there were any truth to the manifestation. He had often warned others not to seek after signs, but to seek Jesus Himself and allow God to give you signs if he so chose to do so.

Another man with a prophetic ministry had pointed him out in a meeting and prophesied that he would be overcome by the Holy Spirit and visited with an unction of the Holy Spirit to the degree that people would not "like your methods." Before 1994 ended, John experienced a sustained touch from God that caused him to appear drunken to people around. Some even confess to being annoyed by the degree to which this display occurred. One well known minister gave him a "word" intended to humiliate him and hopefully, cause him to stop it. John says today that when the Holy Spirit came upon him that he was elevated to ecstasy. It was as though I were "outside myself. There was no sense of gravity with a sense that nothing was hindering me. I was completely free."

To everyone's dismay, John found himself unable to "quit it." He could not "come back to earth" and behave normally as people usually are able to do after receiving a touch from God.

While John was in this state of drunkenness, he would say things that he would not even dare to say had he been sober. These sentences would often single out difficulties in groups and congregations and point out with precise insight that the church was being challenged to accept the unusual. There were times that John extended an altar call in meetings where he had the platform and the altar would be full.

At one conference in Toronto where he was speaking, Heidi Baker, the well-known missionary to Africa, walked into her first meeting ever in Toronto. In this particular meeting, John was "casting" a fishing line out into the audience and spoke of the Holy Spirit as fishing for religious spirits. The Holy Spirit fell upon Heidi in the same way He had with John, and she could not "sober up," either. I was personally in attendance at this meeting and saw it with my own eyes. From that point on, the renewing presence of the Holy Spirit refreshed Heidi so powerfully that she was empowered and emotionally restored. The ministry that Heidi and Rolland have in Africa today gained much strength to continue from the meeting where she was so mightily touched by the Holy Spirit.

John was invited early in this renewal to conferences with other speakers who were more readily subject to what other Pentecostal or charismatic believers accepted as normal. However, as time wore on, he ceased to be invited or even acknowledged by the church "authorities." Invitations dropped off and John was regarded by many people as an outcast, a man who was so drunken that he had somehow "crossed the line." I must confess, as I have already done to John, himself, that I was in the skeptical camp. I did not understand how God would do something like this to someone and cause them to, in effect, lose their ministry.

John says, "I completely understand the negative reactions of other ministers. I had been a pastor myself and would not have known what to do about someone in this state." John was never belligerent, but he was just drunken and not a little bit. He had to withstand threats by airlines who could not tolerate it with the possibility of having his tickets withdrawn.

John says that had it not been for the ecstasy of the Holy Spirit during this time, he could have not survived.

John says that there was no point at which he could say that the unction withdrew, but that gradually he was able to "put two sentences together," whereas before he could not, other than at times to make bold statements about the status quo that were embarrassingly honest.

I talked with John recently in preparation for this new edition of THE RIVER IS HERE. I must say that of all the ministers I have known after having been in the ministry for 50 years, I know of no one more humble and with a gentler spirit than John Scotland. If the fruit of the Spirit is the litmus test of whether or not a manifestation is of God, then what happened to John Scotland was real. The current focus of his ministry is an intimate love relationship with Jesus. I believe that God used John to challenge all of us who thought ourselves yielded to God and yet held bits of ourselves back from Him. John was an example of a man utterly surrendered to the Holy Spirit to the point that he shamelessly took on this work of the Holy Spirit without regard to the fear of man. He was and is truly "not ashamed of the Gospel of Christ."

Church, it is time to celebrate. Like Boaz in Ruth 3:7, the Lord Jesus may be celebrating the beginning of harvest time by causing the body of Christ to be merry. He may want us, for a season preceding the final harvest, to lose our sense false sense of balance and fleshly sense of direction; to cease striving, wailing and fasting, and celebrate a feast to Him.

This generation needs to be strengthened with joy. Nehemiah put an end to the grieving of God's people over having ignored the words of the Law. Excessive sadness, he knew, would demoralize them. So he encouraged them to:

> Go your way, eat the fat, drink the sweet and send portions to those for whom nothing is prepared; for this day is holy to our Lord. Do not sorrow, for the joy of the Lord is your strength. ...And all the people went their way to eat and drink, to send portions and rejoice greatly, because they understood the words that were declared to them. (Nehemiah 8:10,12 NKJV)

Paul told the Ephesians (5:18-19) not only to be baptized with the Holy Spirit but to be filled continuously with the Spirit. This is the secret of abiding in Christ and had they been more careful to drink more deeply of the Holy Spirit, perhaps they would not have left their first love and warranted Jesus' reproof in Revelation 2:4.

Perhaps the residue of this blessing will leave a tradition of being filled with the Holy Spirit constantly.

Resting In The Spirit

Perhaps the most common phenomenon is the vast numbers of those who lie on the floor in response to receiving prayer and then remain on the floor as though soaking in a bath of God's presence. Falling in response to prayer by the laying on of hands of evangelists is nothing new in Pentecostal and Charismatic circles. However, the difference in this renewal is that people who are touched enjoy such a satisfying sense of His Presence that they want to linger in a waiting posture.

It was also a phenomenon apparent in the revivals during the Great Awakening of the 1700s. Jonathan Edwards observed "faintings," as he called them. Wesley, Whitfield and Finney also saw this phenomenon in their meetings. In this century, it is commonly called "being slain in the Spirit" or "going down under the power."

Jonathan Edwards observed in his essay, "Distinguishing Marks of the Work of the Spirit of God," the following:

> So it may easily be accounted for, that a true sense of the glorious excellency of the Lord Jesus Christ, and of His wonderful dying love, and the exercise of a truly spiritual love and joy, should be such as very much to overcome the bodily strength. We are all ready to own that no man can see God and live, and that it is but a very small part of that apprehension of the glory and the love of Christ which the saints enjoy in heaven, that our present frame can bear; therefore, it is not at all strange that God should sometimes give his saints such foretastes of heaven as to diminish their bodily strength. p. 92

The Scriptures describe instances in which individuals were

so overcome with the power of God's presence that they fell. Recall that Abraham "fell on his face" (Genesis 17:17) as he laughed about the promise of Isaac when he was soon to be one hundred years old. Daniel, approached by "the glorious man," wrote that "no strength remained in me" (10:8, NKJV), and he lay with his face to the ground. Ezekiel "fell on his face" as he saw the visions of the four living creatures and "the appearance of the likeness of the glory of the Lord." (1:28) The soldiers and officers who arrested Jesus in the Garden of Gethsemane were overcome by the power of the Holy Spirit as Jesus rose from the place of prayer, and they "fell to the ground." (John 18:6) The Apostle John, exiled on the Isle of Patmos and receiving a vision of the victorious, exalted Christ, "fell at His feet as dead."(Revelation 1:17, NKJV) Saul of Tarsus, confronted by a vision of the Lord on the road to Damascus, "fell to the ground"(Acts 9:4), along with all the men with him (see Acts 26:14) All of these seem to have fallen when confronted by the powerful impact of the presence of God.

There are many scriptures that also indicate that others subjugated themselves to God's Presence voluntarily in order to honor the fact that they knew they were confronted by Someone higher than themselves.

Jairus "fell at Jesus feet" when he implored the Lord to come to his house and heal his daughter. Peter "fell down at Jesus' knees" (Luke 5:8) when he saw the miraculous catch of fish which provoked him to discipleship.

Both of these physical responses—falling under the loss of physical strength and dropping to the floor in worship—seem to be occurring during renewal. Some fall as they sense a wave of power too difficult to resist. Others are yielding to the impact of the voice of God in their spirits or to the awe of a vision they are seeing. Some are choosing to surrender in the same way that others raise their hands.

So what is the good of it? For a time I believed that the Holy Spirit knocked people unconscious for a short time. I was further confused to see people fainting and hopping back up, as though God took delight in seeing if He could push a person over. I had also observed (as I have said earlier) what seemed to be shoving, rocking, pushing or the use of other intimidating means to encourage people to fall. Seeing these things caused me to doubt their validity. Observing the widespread lack of fruit in people's lives from these experiences had also convinced me that they were either false or of little value. I wanted what was real, but I believed the real to be so rare that only an isolated few would experience it.

During these days of renewal, however, I have observed resting in the Spirit as the most common external sign. Frequently those who fall remain on the floor under the influence of the Holy Spirit for periods of minutes to hours. Theologians and students of the revival have commented that to get up too soon is to shortchange a deeper work of the Spirit. Unlike previous times, this phenomenon seems to be occurring widely to those who have previously scorned it or for other reasons never yielded to it.

Drs. Marie and Lowell Hoffman, clinical psychologists practicing in the Lehigh Valley in eastern Pennsylvania, have observed the tendency among those receiving prayer to want to be in a reclining position. The Hoffmanns pointed out to me that Sigmund Freud, known as the father of modern psychology, commented on this fact of human nature in his observations of human psychological response. Human beings, he discovered, were most vulnerable when lying down. For this reason many psychiatrists today still have their patients lie on a couch as they receive counseling. It is no wonder that God may choose to put us into the same position while He is healing our inner man.

Sometimes the person responding in this way to the Holy Spirit's presence has the feeling of being acted on by the power of God that is greater than themselves. John Crane, pastor of Evangelistic Center Church, Kansas City, is more than 6"3" and massive in build. As he received prayer in Toronto, he, too, fell as the Holy Spirit's presence swept over him. This had never happened to him before. As he lay on the floor, he asked, "Lord, is this scriptural?" Immediately the Lord reminded him of the verse, "He makes me lie down in green pastures." (Psalm 23:2)

When sheep lie down in a pasture, they are enjoying a state of contentment and freedom from fear. Perhaps the Lord is placing many of His sheep, like John Crane, in this position to soothe and free them.

Some people want to know if it is right to have someone stand behind the person receiving prayer, since this might encourage them to fall. "If it's God," these people argue, "you don't need a catcher."

I agreed for years, not wanting to promote anything fleshly. But this reason is faulty when we apply it to other things of God. Try these on for size: "If it's God, you don't need anyone to witness to people. If it's God, you don't need to go to the doctor. If God wants you to speak in tongues, you don't need to yield your tongue, the Holy Spirit will do it for you."

For the sake of order, and for protection for those who may go down "in the flesh,"or for those who simply want to yield in order to ensure that they not miss anything the Holy Spirit has for them, it is a good idea to have prayer assistants to stand behind those who are receiving prayer.

If anyone is afraid to fall and feels impressed to lie down, let the sheep lie down in the pasture. What difference does it make in the eternal scheme? What is the worst that could happen? Someone could make a mistake, fall down, get up and serve Jesus anyway. Believe me, the last time you tripped and fell, you fell for much less. What is genuinely wrong with waiting in God's presence however it happens?

No one should be made to feel that he must fall or that he is unspiritual if he does not. Do not compare yourself negatively OR positively with those who fall in response to prayer, and do not prohibit anyone from falling. Give room for the Holy Spirit to do what He wants. After all, as my husband, Bill, likes to say, "It's not about falling; it is about falling in love with Jesus all over again."

Let God Have Control

Allowing the Holy Spirit to move on people freely is one of the big issues in a day of visitation. Whether we understand everything completely or not, we must allow Jesus headship over His Church. This includes setting aside prejudices and fears and giving Him control and authority. In another chapter, I will discuss some of the practical aspects that leaders face. For now, let me say simply that physical manifestations produce awe in a congregation at God's ability to change lives and bring forth fruit. When people see that He is able to move in such a way, it gives them hope for deeper change.

God is stirring the Holy Spirit in people who have allowed gifts to lie dormant for years. Many of the signs occur as the Holy Spirit makes His first powerful move on individuals. The manifestations may not be a permanent fixture in people's spiritual lives. But we must allow the Spirit to move on His people this way as long as He likes. Believers who submit to the Holy Spirit when He moves in this way are permitting the Lord to bring into their lives a further revelation of Himself in this day of visitation. They will certainly begin to lose their inhibitions and fear of man in the middle of it, including in worship, witnessing, serving and manifesting the gifts of the Holy Spirit.

As time goes on, the manifestations may change, deepen in intensity or disappear altogether. Some may remain as keys that open the door to a constant refilling of the Holy Spirit. The deposit the Holy Spirit leaves of joy at the sense of His presence is worth accommodating ourselves to this form of change.

One final word. That some individuals have manifestations and then fall away says nothing about the manifestations. It does say much about them. The power that overcame the guards who arrested Jesus was real, but they did not allow the experience to change their behavior. Judas, too, saw signs and wonders, followed Jesus closely for three years, but he did not allow the experience to make lasting changes in his character. This does not mean that Jesus is not the Son of God. It means that we must allow ourselves to not only be overcome by His power, but we must be changed by His love.

Jesus uses many ways to separate people and even separate followers. I don't want to come to Him only for the "loaves," but I want to be with Him even when I do not understand Him. Do you?

5 - THIS HEALING RIVER

Nick D'Amico is an engineer, a quiet, gentle man married to a vivacious registered nurse named Carol. In 1995, when this book was first written, he and Carol had been beloved members of our congregation for over ten years. While they were with us, they served with the youth and have always been committed to serving the less fortunate and frequently opened their home to the body of Christ, expecting nothing in return.

The new sense of the Lord's presence had not been visiting us long before Nick and Carol presented themselves at the altar one Sunday for prayer. Carol whispered into my ear some unwelcome news. The doctor had discovered a lump on Nick's body. The doctor, also a Christian, had told him plainly that he was concerned and scheduled Nick promptly for a trip to a radiologist at Shadyside Hospital in Pittsburgh.

The D'Amico's faces offered a somber contrast to the laughter coming from the other members at the altar already on the floor under the power of the Spirit. Their news would elicit a serious, concerned response from other more sensitive ministers. But suddenly, without warning, a deep laugh rose up inside me and escaped from my mouth. I heard myself saying, "Well, Honey, this is no problem for God!"

At that moment, Nick and Carol both fell simultaneously to the carpet and began resting in the Spirit.

As I stepped to the next person waiting for prayer, I remember thinking, *why did I just say that?* I had no confidence in my ability to pray for the sick. It has usually seemed that the ones I thought would be healed died, and the scoundrels I thought "deserved" to die got well! Healing had always been and is now a mystery to me.

The next Sunday, however, Nick was one of the first to testify. He had made his trip to the radiologist. As the technologist had scanned the sonogram of Nick's body, he told us, the silence had been deafening.

Oh no, Nick thought, *it must be serious.*

Then the radiologist came in and studied the sonogram himself.

"Mr. D'Amico," he said, "why did your doctors send you here? I can't find anything."

The look on Nick's face as he testified was one of relief and joy. The congregation erupted in laughter, praise and applause, thankful to the Lord Jesus Christ for healing him. The thought that Nick might have contracted a life-threatening illness was something no one had wanted to consider. (*Now, more than 25 years later Nick remains completely healed.)*

Several months later, Nick testified again. He thanked God again for his healing, but he focused his testimony this time on another aspect of the renewal—the healing work God had done inside him. In fact, of the two, Nick prized the internal work of the Spirit as more precious.

Nick D'Amico's healing raised expectations in our church. As the River flowed into the congregation, God renewed our confidence in His healing power and His desire to heal more often. Within a few weeks, we heard four more members testify to healings which were later confirmed by doctors. Surgeries had been canceled, potentially dangerous health problems removed. The Lord was demonstrating His compassion toward us.

We are not the only ones, of course, experiencing this healing river. Throughout the world, the River is producing similar results.

Streams In Rural England

As the renewal began to flow throughout the world in 1994, reports of healings started to circulate. In England renewal has been sweeping the land causing the River to reached beyond cities into rural settings.

Martin Down (1994) is the rector of two neighboring rural Church of England parishes nestled in the countryside of East Anglia in Norfolk, England. On a sunny Sunday morning, he stands robed in his white cassock, waiting at the door of St. George's, whose church bell tower was built in 1497. The churchyard of St. George's is full of grave markers overgrown with deep green grass, some of them leaning, propped up with stones, many inscriptions dating back hundreds of years. The church bells peel out over the sleeping village of Saham Toney—the joyful signal that church is about to begin. Faithful Anglicans begin to make their way into the old flint sanctuary as they have for hundreds of years to sit in ornately carved pews older than the United States of America.

But something new is happening at St.George's. When Martin Down and his wife, Maureen, read about the Toronto Blessing, they journeyed to Ontario hungry for more of God and for His Presence to flow more powerfully into their parishes. They were not disappointed. The river of blessing has been bringing spiritual refreshing to two parishes.

To the question, "How do you know this visitation if of God? Martin replies without hesitation, "The changed lives." Indeed, the congregations are alive with an air of expectancy and simple faith that have been honored by the Holy Spirit's power.

Haley

For three years Haley suffered from anorexia nervosa, the emotional illness that affects many high-achieving young people, causing symptoms of depression and the compulsive desire to starve themselves—sometimes to death. By the time Haley arrived at the spring conference in East Anglia sponsored by Living Waters, a fellowship of renewed Anglicans, in May 1995, she was sullen and wanted nothing more to do with God. She was tired of getting a little better, then becoming worse and receiving no more than temporary help from stays in the hospital. Still, someone prevailed on her, as she attended the youth event to get prayer and let God come in and take control.

On the second day of the conference, Haley decided to give the Lord a chance. She came forward for prayer at the end of one of the meetings.

As someone prayed for her, she fell to the floor with the sensation that God was punching her in the stomach. All night long her body jerked and she "grunted," continuing to feel "punches." The following day, Haley received more prayer, only to have the manifestation continue.

But the Lord took away the anorexia, filled her with His Spirit and restored her appetite. Since May 1995, Haley has been free of symptoms. the Lord did more for her in a few hours than anyone else had been able to do in years of counseling.

Another woman who had been incapacitated with excruciating back pain for which medication brought no relief, found the pain disappear completely as she received soaking prayer. Prayer enabled her to function normally again.

Emotional Healing

In our congregation, the healing power of the Lord Jesus Christ found a new dimension of release within weeks after members began receiving prayer. The furrowed brows and downcast countenances that had once stared back at Bill and me as we stood behind the pulpit were being changed into mirrors of newfound peace.

"The Hot Flash Club"

The summer of 1994 was difficult emotionally for several of us women. I had endured a hysterectomy and complications that resulted in infections. Then, as my estrogen level took an unexpected, dramatic drop, I was plunged into hormone shock, which resulted in panic attacks. These exacted a painful toll from my already discouraged emotions. I would wake up at night trembling in terror, as though something awful were about to happen to me. The fear of disease—a fear from which the Lord had mercifully freed me twenty years before started - pressing in on me again.

I had once been a fun-loving, positive person. Now, shell-shocked by the trauma of surgery and the tragedies that surrounded me in the lives of other church members, I felt the devastation of mental agony. At times I thought I would lose my mind.

However, after several months of soaking in God's presence repeatedly, the Lord gradually lifted the darkness and replaced it with tranquility and joy.

I was not the only one suffering. Several other women in the congregation had been suffering depression and fear also as a result of the natural onset of the change of life. When we discovered that we were all suffering similar emotional and physical symptoms, we decided to form a support group and meet for dinner in a nice restaurant once a month, in the hopes that talking about it would help. We informally dubbed ourselves "The Hot Flash Club."

Not long after renewal began, I noticed the entire Hot Flash Club down on the carpet at the altar one night under the influence of the Holy Spirit. Everyone of them was engaged with the Lord and experiencing waves of peace and joy washing over their previously tormented emotions.

Shirley Nardina, one of the most faithful women in our congregation and a member of the Hot Flash Club, had not smiled much in three years—at least, not with her heart. As the the Holy Spirit fell on Shirley, she began to be transformed by the laughter. In her mind's eye, as she testified later, she saw Heaven open up and caught a glimpse of the atmosphere there. Heaven she saw, was in a constant state of rejoicing. Suddenly aware of the victory we have in Christ, she felt like shouting praises to Jesus, but out of her mouth came the words, "Hip, hip hooray! Three cheers for Jesus!"—for more than two hours. She felt a renewed sense of the love of God for her. As she lay on the floor laughing and praising Him, she realized that some parishioners on the floor around her were also exulting in the Lord. She sensed the love of God lifting everyone out of misery.

Several months later, Shirley's husband, Ron, had to give up his job because of heart problems. For several days Shirley felt anxiety about the future beginning to press in on her. One night she awoke with the strongest anxiety attack she had had—much stronger that the ones she had experienced before the renewal. Despite much prayer and a sense of victory how she felt swallowed up, overwhelmed by spiritual battle.

Then into her left ear she heard a song, a new melody she had never heard before, and the words *God will take care of you.* For two hours, it seemed that an angel was singing to her. Her prayer had been answered. Peace returned.

In church on December 17, 1995, just a week before Christmas, Shirley's husband, Ron, presented the pastors' Christmas gifts from the congregation. Ron had built a model of our church building, covered it with silver wrapping paper and fixed it so the roof could be removed. He talked about the peace God had given him during the renewal, recounted the joys and sorrows the congregation had faced during the year and thanked the pastors on behalf of everyone for their labors of love. Then he sat down in the pew next to Shirley.

As Bill opened the Bible and began his message, suddenly Ron slumped over onto his wife. Without a sign of pain, he went to be with the Lord.

Shirley grieved through periods of extreme sadness. The thought that her beloved husband of 29 years had gone was almost impossible to bear. But as she shared her emotional pain with me, Shirley said "each day, as my missing Ron grows stronger and stronger, my love for God and His people and my desire to serve Him, are growing greater at the same time. I have no doubt that had Ron passed away before the renewal, I may have become bitter at God and could not have had the strength to go through this."

Although she shared it with no one at the time, Shirley was aware that whenever the Lord filled her mouth with laughter, it was strengthening her for what was to come.Though she did not admit it to herself, deep inside she knew that God was going to take Ron home.

"What if I had not responded to the renewal?" Shirley remarked to me. "What if I had not been willing to receive prayer? I don't know how I would have lived through this had it not been for the strength God has given me in this renewal."

Repeated fillings of the Holy Spirit have brought Shirley comfort in her grief—and have revived the dashed hopes of the other women as well. They found a new confidence in the power of God to bless their futures by working all things together for their good.

Once They Were Blind, Now They See

One Sunday morning during congregational worship, Jim Arth, who had retired recently from his job, began to weep loudly as everyone else was singing. This was unlike affable Jim, who often teased the people he loved; no one thought he had a care in the world. The following Sunday Jim testified that the presence of the Lord had surrounded him during worship and lifted a depression he had concealed from everyone. It has not returned.

The move of the Spirit not only affected older adults, but younger ones as well.

Missy was a college student who grew up in our congregation since her mother came to Christ more than twelve years before the outpouring of the Holy Spirit. Missy's parents were divorced. Living without her dad around the house and not being able to experience fatherly affection caused Missy to pay a heavy emotional price. She experienced depression, suffered from low self-esteem and felt like an outsider. At times she even felt suicidal.

Missy soaked in the presence of the Lord, receiving prayer at every service. During the ministry time, she would often lie on the carpet, smiling peacefully or be filled with laughter. As her inner healing began, she began to "see" herself on the lap of her Heavenly Father surrounded by His arms of love while they watched a sunset together.

She could not believe at first that her Heavenly Father was taking time just to be with her. Once she remarked to Him how beautiful the sunset was. The Lord responded, *Everything I make is beautiful, including you. You are My precious child and I love you.*

As God began to restore her wounded soul, Missy's blue eyes began to shine as He restored her self-confidence. As her healing progressed, she began to bring her flute to church and play for her Heavenly Father. During the altar service as people received prayer, she played her flute over them spontaneously as a shepherd would play over his sheep in a field. Before, she was too shy to play in front of others. Once Missy was blind to the Father's love; now she sees. (see John 9:25)

Linda is a women's leader in a church in Bethlehem, PA. Since she was a child, she habitually bit her fingernails. Sometimes her fingers were sore and painful, her nails bitten almost to the quick.

When Linda accompanied her pastor's wife, Tricia Groblewski, to services in Toronto she wanted to receive prayer to take in whatever God had for her. As a member of the prayer team prayed for her, she dropped to the floor, her arms began to flail about and her head began to shake. Her body bounced on the floor so violently that she testified later to carpet burns on her elbows! Yet she sensed God's presence, without understanding what specifically He had done for her. She felt that something had been removed, as if she had had laser surgery.

Two weeks later, shampooing her hair in the shower, she felt her head being gently scratched. She looked down to see that her nails had grown out full-length past the ends of her fingers for the first time in her life!

At the fall women's retreat, Linda dangled her manicured nails over the pulpit as she testified to the inner healing the Lord had given her. She still does not know what God touched inside her; she only knows that He touched the inner anxiety which was at root of her nail-biting.

Irene Bell, wife of one of Britain's renewal leaders, Stuart Bell, was always reticent to speak in public places. Standing before any group, even in her own church, paralyzed her with fear. Whenever the possibility existed that someone might call her to the front, Irene spent anxious hours worrying about it, fearing what might happen if she opened her mouth and nothing came out, or if she said something wrong. If there was the slightest possibility that she might be called on, even to say grace before a meal, sometimes she excused herself.

But something happened to Irene through months of receiving prayer and being filled with the Holy Spirit. Not long ago she and Stuart were gathered together for a meal with some of Britain's leaders and their wives, Gerald Coates asked Irene to say grace. Rather than being overtaken by the usual panic, she said to herself, *Well, why not?* She opened her mouth and to her husband's surprise, prayed aloud in front of everyone. She has since testified before her own church of her healing which remains to this day, over 26 years later.

In Acts 4 the entire church prayed for boldness:

And when they had prayed, the place where they were assembled together was shaken; and they were all filled with the Holy Spirit, and they spoke the word of God with boldness. (Acts.4:31 NKJV)

Perhaps you need a touch from the Holy Spirit to break through your own wall of fear. God can do it!

He Restores My Soul

Because Jesus Christ is the Good Shepherd David prophesied about in Psalm 23, any move of the Holy Spirit will accomplish, with God's power, the tasks of a faithful caretaker of the flock. If the current move is really a prelude to widespread revival, it is for the good of the Church. He is leading His flock gently to quiet waters and green pastures where they can be cleansed, watered and fed. The Lord is more grieved than we are, I believe, over the devastation that many of His sheep are experiencing. So the overwhelming sight of these sheep lying in large groups in His presence is enough to revive the hope of any pastor of His flock.

One of my principle concerns for several years has been the emotional state of God's people. How can a child of the Heavenly Father, limping through life with unhealed emotional wounds, or devastated by grief over disappointed hopes, help to gather in a harvest of souls in a time of revival? Many suffering sheep today are bearing witness to the dimension of the Holy Spirit's power to bind up the broken-hearted that has been missing in the Church.

At at a conference in Toronto in October 1995, as I lay on the floor, I felt an unusual sense of the Lord's soothing presence. I "saw" myself coming upon a wounded man lying by the road in the middle of a wilderness. Feeling compassion for him, I began scanning the surroundings looking for raw materials to bind up his wounds. I found a crudely shaped stick and bound his arm with a scrap of cloth torn from something I had with me. I sat beside the man, my eyes scanning the horizon anxiously waiting for help to arrive.

Even as I lay on the floor, the Holy Spirit gave me the interpretation:

There are many like you who could not pass the wounded by. You are like the Good Samaritan, who did the best he could with what he had; but a day is coming when what you have been able to do for people now will seem like applying first aid. You will see help from the throne of God, a powerful anointing of the Lord to do what you have to this moment only wished you could.

In that moment I experienced a release of guilt that had been projected onto me by the criticism and misunderstanding from others in the body of Christ. I realized that I had not grieved the Lord, but that He knew I knew I had confidence in Him. The only thing I did not know was how long it would take Him to arrive.

Are these healings significant? Ask those who are being healed. Do they attribute the healings to Jesus Christ? What does the presence of healing mean? Nothing—unless the healings glorify the God and Father of our Lord Jesus Christ. This is how we know the Holy Spirit is at work.

Some say that we should not trust that form of evidence—implying that unless something is totally traditional and appears letter for letter in Scripture, it could not possible produce anything godly. But this is the attitude the Pharisees had when Jesus healed people on the Sabbath. Disregarding the presence of His awesome power, they quibbled over whether it was scriptural. When the man lame for 38 years picked up his bed and walked away from the portico of the pool of Bethesda, the Pharisees wanted to know if this was a scriptural manifestation. But the Lord Himself told us to believe Him for His works' sake:

> If I do not do the works of My Father, do not believe Me; but if I do them, though you do not believe Me, believe the works, that you may know and understand that the Father is in Me, and I in the Father. (John 10:37-38)

If the miracles of inner healing we are now seeing take place on a widespread scale are a harbinger of things to come, we need to prepare ourselves to see God's power make our crude methods obsolete. I wonder how we will react if the day comes when God's children do not need our help anymore! I think I will be glad!

But not only does the Lord heal to relieve the sufferings of His children. In addition, manifestations of the healing power of God draw attention to the fact that He is moving, as happened in Debra Petrosky's life.

The Children's Bread

An hour before the first service of our renewal weekend in August 1995, Debra Petrosky arrived early to make sure she got a seat.

An articulate, professional woman, freelance writer and editor, Debra serves on the worship team of her congregation. Three years before, on a day she had set aside for prayer and fasting, a car accident disrupted her life. A teenager with a new driver's license cut across her path as she drove through a green light. Both vehicles were totaled.

After the accident she saw an orthopedic doctor, a physical therapist and a chiropractor for help with her injuries. Accustomed to an active life, Debra was dismayed to discover that just a few minutes of walking now caused debilitating headaches. Sometimes she took ten to twelve Tylenol a day, and needed to lie down frequently to take the pressure off her neck. This put a crunch on her home-based business she had just started, and her income plummeted. The chronic pain and the loss of income contributed to depression.

The Holy Spirit touched Debra's life dramatically in June 1995, when she visited another congregation in our area. The pastor and his wife had just returned from Toronto. During the ministry time at her church, Debra fell under the power of the Spirit and found that her long-standing depression had lifted.

Then came our August renewal weekend. At the conclusion of the Friday evening service, we stacked the chairs and asked those who wanted prayer to stand to receive ministry. As a member of the ministry team laid hands on Debra, she fell to the carpet and found her arms moving back and forth. As the sense of God's power increased, her head began to shake vigorously from side to side.

She thought *Lord, I hope this is my healing. If it's not, I'm going to be really sore tomorrow!*

Her physical manifestations lasted nearly an hour. Checking her neck, Debra noticed that the muscles were unusually supple.

At home after the meeting, she noticed an odd-shaped crust of bread a few inches below her pillow. She had not eaten in her bedroom and did not know where it had come from. As she popped the morsel into her mouth, a scripture passage dropped into her mind, one she had read during her devotional time that very morning. It was the passage where the Canaanite woman begged Jesus to heal her daughter (see Matthew 15:22-28). Jesus had told the woman, "It is not good to take the children's bread and throw it to the dogs" (verse 26). The woman replied to Jesus, "Yes, Lord; but even the dogs feed on the crumbs which fall from their master's table" (verse 27). Debra began to wonder if she, too, had begun to take the divine crumbs.

The next morning, Saturday, she went to the track to walk. As she finished her fourth lap—her limit since the accident—she felt the Lord say, *Take a victory lap!* She began to run. Checking her neck over the next half-mile, she began to say aloud, "I've got the children's bread! I'm healed!" She traveled another mile —running, walking and rejoicing all the way. As hour after hour passed with no stiffness and no headache, she realized that she had been miraculously healed.

On Sunday, the power of the Holy Spirit descended on Debra again in her own church. As the worship team pray and before the service, she became "drunk" in the Spirit and fell to the floor. The others who were standing in for the pastor who was on vacation, did not know what to think. But knowing Debra to be stable and mature they "handled" the scene as best they could.

But it was too late. The curiosity of all who knew her was irreversibly pricked, and the Holy Spirit kindled renewal fire in her local church.

Renewal Of Gifts Of Healing

Nancy Westerberg, the quiet, reserved children's pastor who asked me to dance with her in church, made a scheduled trip to the gynecologist a few days after the Holy Spirit fell on her. One cyst in her breast, which had been monitored for four years, had already been removed surgically. Now she learned she had another one, which had been monitored for two years, had suddenly disappeared.

Encouraged to see the power of God move in her own body Nancy began to lay hands on her husband each night as he slept. Bert had been scheduled for the surgical removal of a large cyst on his leg, which had caused him to limp for more than a year. Nothing had helped; surgery was thought to be the only solution for him. But every night as Nancy prayed, the cyst gradually disappeared and Bert's surgery was canceled.

Ruth Madeira, a breakfast waitress at a local coffee shop, heard about the moving of the Spirit from Bill and me as she waited on our table. Ruth began to visit our church and receive prayer. Joy returned to her life. Then, a few weeks later, she failed a stress test during her yearly physical. The doctor feared her arteries were blocked. But as Ruth continued to soak in prayer at the altar, the Lord gave her an overwhelming sense of peace. We were all thrilled when her angiogram showed she did not need surgery.

As a new surge of healing power flows through the Church, the Body of Christ is beginning to pray for the sick more often, simply asking the Holy Spirit to come as He chooses.

Recently a young teenager, Tiffany Sines, who participates in our church puppet ministry serving nursing homes, fell on the step at church, her ankle began to swell immediately. Carol, our "resident R.N," feared a torn ligament. Members of the church including kids playing nearby, gathered around her for prayer. Then her mother loaded her into the car and headed for the emergency room.

As they approached the hospital, Tiffany looked at her ankle and asked her mother to pull over by the side of the road. The swelling had gone down completely. Bouncing up and down in excitement, Tiffany put her shoe back on, went back to church and helped the puppet ministry that very afternoon.

Carol, the nurse, told me later that she knew Tiffany's ankle had been seriously injured and that there was no way it could have naturally repaired itself in that short a time.

Before renewal broke out in our congregation, praying for the sick had become perfunctory, something we did I because we knew it was right. God honored it anyway, but many folks we prayed for seemed to experience nothing. Every so often someone would improve, but we could not tell if it was the natural healing process of the miraculous power of the Holy Spirit. Even natural healing is a blessing from God, but when people became seriously ill, we had little faith to pray for them.

Not all have been healed who have suffered physical problems since the renewal began; but even those who have not have found renewed strength to stand and face the trial with a sense of God's tender, watchful care rather than feeling abandoned in their hour of need.

Whenever I pray, "More, Lord" these days, one of my desires is for more demonstrations of His healing power and that He will continue to open my eyes to see them!

How Can I Experience His Healing?

The healing power of God that comes is in direct response to the cries of His children for more of their heavenly Father's presence in their lives. The healings have come by His sovereignty as He is given the opportunity to touch each one and bring whatever manifestation He chooses.

At the same time, there is much scriptural support for beseeching the Lord specifically to heal. If healing is an important concern for you, continue to receive prayer as often as possible and continue to respond to the inner promptings of the Holy Spirit. But continue to set aside your own agenda. You may not remember that your Heavenly Father knows what you have need of before the request leaves your lips. (See Matthew 6:8) So keep asking for more of Him, and do not be surprised when you sense His healing power flowing through you; or when you discover, perhaps without feeling anything at all at the moment it happens, that your ailment or disease is gone.

Pray for others to be healed, too, asking the Lord especially to come upon them in the way He desires. Since we were set free over 45 years ago from the heresy of cessationism, the false doctrine that miracles were only for the first century church, we have always prayed for the sick. In over 45 years in pastoral ministry we have seen the Lord do marvelous works and have a far healthier congregation than had we decided that God does not heal today. Jesus Christ is still "the same yesterday, today and forever." (Hebrews 13: 8)

During seasons of refreshing and revival, the Lord visits His people with signs and wonders for the purpose of restoring their awe with demonstrations of His merciful power. All He needs is room to move. Give Him every opportunity to do so.

Now let's look at how you and your congregation can open the doors of the local church to His blessing and cooperate with the Lord to fan the flames into full-scale awakening!

6 - PREPARING TO RECEIVE THE BLESSING

Receiving the blessing of renewal is like jumping into a river and allowing yourself to be carried along. But what if you are afraid of the water? Paul Blackham (chapter 4) testified before the congregation after being touched by the Lord, "I wasn't afraid that it wasn't God; I was afraid that it was, and that I would have to face Him."

The fear of facing God and of perhaps being passed over by Him haunts many of God's children. A visitation from the Lord is a precious time, a time when he seems to bend down and kiss the earth, drawing near to His children and to the lost world. But it is estimated that nearly one quarter of those in every congregation fear they will find themselves remaining in their seats, or even standing for prayer and receiving nothing while everyone else gets blessed. Why do many of us believe God will pass us by?

Sometimes the excuses we make-especially our theological ones-are just covers for fear. Maybe you will have trouble admitting that you are *afraid.* But preparing your heart to receive the blessing of renewal necessitates taking a look at the reasons you may be afraid.

Before the flood, Noah had to spend time building the ark. Before the Lord came in glory to Israel, they had to build the tabernacle. God told Elisha that Jehoshaphat was to make the valley full of ditches. Elisha told the widow without found or resources to borrow vessels from her neighbor: "Do not get a few." (2 Kings 4:3) He promised that her jar of oil would be multiplied to fill every vessel.

The point is, before God moves, He often asks us to prepare.

Prepare To Contain The Blessing

In the late '70's, Elliott Tepper, close friend, missionary and founder of Betel International which is headquartered in Madrid, Spain, visited our congregation with his wife, Mary. He prophesied, "Prepare to contain the blessing..." We did not know that in 1994, a move of the Spirit would break out in Toronto called "the blessing" and "the river." Nor did we know we would be involved. We even made a banner and hung it on the wall behind the pulpit to remind us to ready ourselves for what God would do. But it is difficult to prepare for something unseen and unknown. All we could do was surrender to the Holy Spirit's leading day after day (some days more successfully than others).

In 1986, Bill and I became involved in the Christian recovery movement, which was addressing the emotional pain and other effects on those who had grown up in homes with alcoholism and abuse. I remember how shocked we were to find that ninety per cent of the members of our own congregation fell into this category! Many of our brothers and sisters were suffering and we had not even realized it. Many lived without being able to experience love. Still others suffered secretly from addictions they felt were too shameful to disclose in a Christian setting.

As Bill and I began to study to gain a practical knowledge about the human soul, we began to see how our own lives had been affected by our childhood experiences. Although our families were different from theirs, we shared many of the same emotional inhibitions. I have written several other books sharing about these issues. But I did not realize until the blessings of renewal came how the Lord had been carrying me through a healing process as part of a chain of preparatory events leading to the next chapter in my Christian maturity, part of which has come through renewal. The knowledge I was gaining about my emotional weaknesses would help me learn not to quench the Holy Spirit, but rather to fan His flame in my soul.

In chapter 2 we observed how we can miss a move of the Holy Spirit when we cherish preconceived notions of what revival should be like.

John Arnott, founding pastor of the fellowship in Toronto, was disturbed early in the outpouring because his own idea of revival included numerous commitments to Christ. He began to try to direct the flow toward the lost. When he did, however, he sensed a struggle and felt as though he may have been resisting the Holy Spirit. When he prayed about it, the Lord spoke in terms he could understand: *Is it all right with you if I 'love up' on My Church for awhile?*

We who tend to place a higher value on results than God does (like the Ephesians church in the book of Revelation) will see little value in the current blessing. In this framework, every move of God is measured by the number of grains of wheat in the harvest.

What is happening now, by contrast, is the Holy Spirit's work to renew in Jesus' bride a deep love for Him that will become the underlying motivation for all future work. Bill believes that out of this move of God will come an army of happy missionaries to gather in the waiting harvest out of love for Him. Enjoying what God is doing now depends on your ability to open the shut-off valve of your heart and let Him love you. We cannot be fruitful without receiving His love.

According to Jonathan Edwards, revival is manifested on two fronts: the salvation of sinners and the quickening of the saints. What we are seeing now is a quickening of our love for Jesus that makes our countenances glow and causes the world to take notice. Fresh oil is being poured into empty lamp stands.

But what if there are subconscious hindrances to our being able to receive love? What prevents us from being able to receive?

Letting God Touch You

The apostle Peter, one of Jesus' closest friends and disciples, found it difficult at first to receive from Jesus. He was happy to have been chosen to follow Him, but was certain up until Jesus' crucifixion that his selection was based on the fact that the Lord needed him. Peter refused to believe he was capable of denying Jesus, and in the Garden of Gethsemane pulled out his sword to provide Jesus with security services.

Everyone is amused at times by the blustering, ingenuous sayings and deeds of Peter. We all know people like him who vocally express every observation that comes to mind and have the entire Christian walk analyzed and condensed into pithy quips. We may not recognize that we are like Peter in our unwillingness to present ourselves for ministry because receiving from the Lord is harder for us than serving Him.

During the Last Supper, Jesus performed a humbling act of affection and service for His most trusted friends. After dinner He laid aside His cloak, placed a towel around His waist and began to wash the feet of each disciples. They had walked with Him faithfully for three years and given up everything to follow Him. Now, as He offered them an act of love and a model for their future treatment of one another, everyone cooperated—except Peter. When Jesus reached him, Peter withdrew his feet. After all, he was one of the closest disciples and devoted to his Master. What Jesus was doing made no sense.

But Jesus shocked him with His insistence. "What I do you do not realize now, but you shall understand hereafter." (John 13:7) It is not necessary, in other words, to understand what God is doing. All we need to know is that Jesus wants to touch us.

But Jesus went further. "If I do not wash you, you have no part with Me." (*No* in the Greek means *no.*)

Jesus was doing something new to each of His disciples, something He had never done before. It may have been embarrassing and uncomfortable emotionally. Obviously they did not understand it. But unless they allowed Him to do what He wanted to, they could have no part of ministry with Him.

Giving out in ministry is directly proportional to our willingness and ability to receive from Jesus. It does not matter if you are one of His closest disciples, have a dynamic and powerful ministry or hold a position of 'authority' in the Body of Christ; if the Lord tells you to reach out your foot, do it! Regardless of our realm of responsibility or place of dignity, we desperately need His touch.

Surely the word *dignity* was epitomized in the late David Edwards, president emeritus of Elim Bible Institute in Lima, New York. He held a prominent place among Charismatic and Pentecostal leaders and was an elder of Elim Fellowship, Lima, NY, one of the oldest and most respected Pentecostal streams in the world, overseeing churches and pastors in many countries. When David taught, he articulated profound insight with a Welsh accent, and his gracious demeanor, tall stature and silver-white hair and beard created an imposing presence.

His first contact with the renewal came through the ministry of Rodney Howard-Browne at the Carpenter's Home Church in Lakeland, Florida. "The longer I watched him," David recounted, "the more convinced I became of his integrity." As David and his wife, Mefus, drove to Elim the week after for their annual conference, he stopped in North Carolina and happened to purchase Jack Hayford's book, *Desire for Fullness.*

"I was quite convicted by what he had to say," David continues. "I had to ask myself whether I was as eager and strenuous in my pursuit of all that God had for me as I had been before I retired. I recognized this as another wave of renewal that God was sending His Church. I prayed and said, *Lord, I don't want to be on the sidelines. I don't want to be a spectator. I certainly don't want to be a critic.* It is often said that those most likely to be hostile toward a renewal are those who were last affected by a visitation from God. I certainly didn't want that to happen to me."

Of the fifteen meetings at Elim that week, David was able to attend thirteen. He stood for prayer at every one, but he did not seem to receive the blessing he sought.

"Eventually," he explained, "more by accident than anything, I was accosted by a 'catcher' who asked him, 'would you like to be prayed for?' I didn't have the courage to say no."

It was then that the power of God began to touch David Edwards. He fell to the floor under the power of the Holy Spirit. That created an "earthquake" sending aftershocks throughout the Elim Fellowship. Phones started ringing all over the Elim Fellowship internationally. David Edwards never fell in response to prayer nor had he exhibited anything in the way of outward manifestations. His ability to receive from God was the "sign" that many needed to receive themselves.

The reaction of a man like David Edwards to the current (1994) wave of the renewal demonstrates how we should respond to Jesus' desire to touch our lives in a new way: with keen discernment, earnest longing, continual searching and humble submission. If what we see moving through the Church today is truly a work of the Spirit, we must acknowledge it and honor the desire of the Lord Jesus to touch us personally with His Holy Spirit. If Jesus is showing up in the Church to touch His bride with an outpouring of His Spirit, we must acknowledge it and honor the desire of the Lord Jesus to touch us personally with His Holy Spirit. We must find a way to allow Him the utmost liberty to do so.

Jonathan Edwards in "Distinguishing Marks of the Word of the Spirit of God" said it this way:

Now Christ is come down from heaven in a remarkable and wonderful work of his Spirit, it becomes all his professed disciples to acknowledge Him and give Him honor. (*Edwards on Revival*, p. 130)

Why Is Receiving Difficult?

What are some of the hindrances to our being able to receive the love of God?

"I Don't Understand It"

Perhaps Peter's reason for withdrawing his feet from the hands of Jesus is the same reason you have difficulty: You do not understand what He is doing. Some people feel the must understand and analyze everything before they embrace or surrender to it.

This is funny, when you think about it. We cannot grasp the mysteries of God—mysteries like salvation, the Trinity, His love for us sinners and many others. We accept them by faith. If we lived to be a thousand, we would not comprehend a thimbleful of God in comparison to what He knows.

Even so, each child of God receives the new birth before he or she understands much of it; and it is necessary to become childlike in order to receive anything from God. "Unless you are converted and become like children," said Jesus, "you shall not enter the kingdom of heaven." (Matthew 18:3) Children do not need to understand and analyze in order to appreciate. They simply relish the moment. In fact, the mystery is part of the wonder of the moment for them.

Jesus explained patiently to Peter at the Last Supper what we *all* need to hear. We may not understand what He wants to do for each of us in this renewal as we receive prayer and a touch from His Spirit, but we must open our hearts to Him and let Him do what He wants.

Fear Of Receiving A False Spirit

The fear of being deceived by a false spirit is a major hindrance to many earnest Christians. Paul warned that in the last days "some will fall away from the faith, paying attention to deceitful spirits and doctrines of demons." (I Timothy 4:1) It is such a concern that there are many so-called "ministries" devoted to rooting out false doctrines and calling out the names of people who preach what they have deemed to be "heresy," as though believers should be frightened of unwittingly receiving the false.

Every spirit yields some kind of fruit, but the fruit of a wrong spirit is as obvious as the fruit of the Holy Spirit. A wrong spirit causes you to fear and leads you away from trusting God. The Holy Spirit causes a person to love God, deny selfishness and love people. A wrong spirit fears, mistrusts, rebels and hardens the heart. Neither suspicion nor intelligence can protect a person from a false spirit. Perhaps you have seen people who have been gradually seduced away from Christ and the truth by trusting their own analysis.

The night before we went to Toronto the first time, a woman approached my husband to warn him that if we went to Toronto to "that church" we would be in danger of receiving a false spirit. She had been a fan of a radio "teacher" who felt it was his duty to expose what was going on in Toronto as deception. He had never been to Toronto, did not know anyone there but from afar had judged it. Unfortunately, thousands of Christians listened to his false spirit and never availed themselves of the blessing of God there because they were afraid they would be deceived.

When you are seeking the Lord, Jesus promised that like a child asking bread from his own father, you will not receive a stone nor a serpent; but if you ask for the Holy Spirit, you will receive Him. (Luke 11: 10-13)

Think of the woman with the issue of blood, elbowing her way through the crowd, just to touch the hem of Jesus' garment. The Pharisees had been warning everyone to stay away from Jesus' meetings because he was a deceiver. They even accused him of having a demon. She literally pushed and shoved her way to Jesus. She was not concerned about the motives of the people around her nor whether or not anyone in the crowd had a false spirit. She knew that if she just touched the hem of His garment, she would be healed. Are you seeking Jesus? Then the Holy Spirit will protect you from everything false because of the purity and simplicity of your expectation to receive from Him.

During the Charismatic renewal, many honest seekers who wanted so desperately to receive the baptism in the Holy Spirit were afraid to allow themselves to pray with their spirits (as opposed to praying with their understanding) because of this fear. I remember seeking for months, going to different meeting and receiving prayer from various pastors. Finally, when I heard some teenage boys praying with their spirits, I mustered the courage to let go and allow myself to speak something I had never learned.

A few months later, the Lord confirmed the gift. I was in Dallas, TX at the altar of Beverly Hills Baptist Church in the fall of 1973. I felt an urge to start praying in the spirit without regard to how it sounded. I just knew I had to.

A few hours later after I returned home, I received a call from my sister who was in Lubbock, several hundred miles away. She had been praying unbeknownst to me that night to receive the baptism in the Holy Spirit. She was rejoicing over the phone, speaking in tongues. I realized then that I had the "real deal;" I had been praying for her without knowing it! God confirmed my experience months after I had stepped out in faith and begun to speak in a language I had never learned. Sometimes, God works that way. I trusted Him first and He confirmed it later.

How often do we place more confidence in Satan to give us a false spirit than we place in our Heavenly Father and His Holy Spirit to "lead us into all truth?"

Fears of various kinds, though, do prevent seekers from going forward. Let's look at some of them.

Fear Of Getting Into The Flesh

Why do we never ask when we are about to gossip, *I wonder if I'm getting into the flesh*? It's only when we might be "guilty" of not yielding to the Holy Spirit. The Holy Spirit works through the natural man like a fountain springing up cleaning out the debris at first as the pure water begins to flow. The Holy Spirit leads us only through our natural selves, the flesh. The scripture admonishes us to yield our "members," in other words, "our flesh" to Him. Everything God does through you will be by your "flesh" cooperating with God. Don't be put off by this one. Yield your "members" as servants who are alive from the dead. Let go and receive. Do not resist the Holy Spirit and quench Him.

Tell the Lord your fears and anxieties. Be honest with Him about them, but tell Him that you are going to yield and trust Him. Ask Him to confirm the validity of your experiences. He knows you and remembers that you are "but dust," according to Isaiah.

A core of selfishness is at the heart of the works of the flesh. They are anger, wrath, malice, lust and greed; but the Holy Spirit's fruit are love, joy, peace, patience, kindness, gentleness, meekness, self-control. If you are pursuing a life truly led by the Holy Spirit and are desiring to have these qualities, you are not "getting into the flesh;" but instead, seeking God.

God loves you and is happy when you are pursuing Him. What is the root of your actions? When you are desiring more of Him and to be soft and pure in heart, it is the Lord who is leading you and motivating your actions. Those kinds of desires do not come from the "flesh."

A Fear Of Emotional Reactions

The fear of emotional reactions is another difficulty that prevents some sincere Christians from receiving a touch from God. They are convinced that the Lord will "explode" within them and cause them to behave in a manner contrary to their judgment. They often quote this verse: "Let all things be done decently and in order." (I Corinthians 14:40 KJV) The apostle Paul, however (contrary to the assumptions of these Bible-quoting Christians), believed in allowing the Holy Spirit to reign in the Church. Let's not sacrifice "let all things be done" on the altar of "decently and in order."

When we feel uncomfortable with someone's emotional intensity, we tend to use our own feelings as the thermometer for judging the validity of their experience. Numerous times in this renewal, my own comfort zone has been invaded by people who became what I thought to be "too emotional." But the Scriptures are full of people who carried on in the presence of Jesus Christ.

Some responded emotionally with shouting or crying out for mercy. Others invaded parties or went to great lengths to get His attention. Jesus rebuked demons, but in no case did He rebuke a single person for an emotional outburst. (Rather, it is the church devoid of the emotion of love whom Jesus rebuked in Revelation 2:4-5.)

Our emotions were given to us by God to enable us to enjoy His fullness and find release from the tension that comes when we feel very deeply. The more vulnerable we are, the more open we will be emotionally. Humility and vulnerability go together. It makes no sense to purport that the the fullness of the Holy Spirit which Paul equates with deep joy, drunkenness, groanings too deep for words and the unfathomable riches of Christ—can be experienced without emotion. Living in the Spirit does involve the emotions (as well as the mind and will) and is designed to make an impact that will last forever.

Jesus as Lord of your life has the right over your emotions as He does every other part of you.

Then the next one is one of the foremost "quenchers" of the Holy Spirit!

Fear Of Losing Control

The group with the greatest difficulty receiving is the one that stands as sentinels in the Church: the Lord's ministers.

One of the curious things I noticed about the services in Toronto was the large number of pastors from all over the globe. It is difficult for a pastor to be touched in his or her own church. The responsibility of making sure everyone else is receiving, and the habit of being selfless in every service, inhibit a pastor's opportunities to receive. Then there are the expectations of others, many of which are unrealistic, who are quick to criticize the pastor if he fails to meet them or if he is seen in an undignified pose. And finally, pastors are generally possessed with a need to control. (I speak from personal experience-!)

Other members of the Body of Christ who have grown up in homes where violence, abuse or lack of nurturing made them feel insecure are also preoccupied (subconsciously or otherwise) with the need to control their environments. They are used to managing situations and to organizing everyone into disciplined regiments. Some people who are natural born managers believe they are called and gifted by God to administer every arena in which they find themselves. More than once, since my own responsibility on the pastoral staff of our church has been to administer, I have become preoccupied with organizing renewal meetings and have heard the Lord say, *Let Me love you.*

One of the first lessons of a disciple is to give up one's own agenda in favor of His. God tests your willingness to do this by things He asks you to do that violate your dignity and right to control your environment. Arrogance in a situation is one of the chief symptoms of the fear of losing control. Forging ahead without humble consideration of what He wants coupled with an attitude that causes you to believe you know how God acts and how He wants to deal with others readily manifest in a challenging situation like the ones you will face in the renewal.

Relinquishing control of a situation in which ministry is occurring, and then actually receiving a blessing yourself, is foreign to pastors who may only have two weeks of vacation per year, much less fewer opportunities to travel to receive ministry themselves. Even when a pastor is on retreat, they are generally in learning mode, looking for ways to make the church grow or for new recipes for serving the Scriptures to hungry sheep. Many ministers find it more comfortable in spiritual situations where they are required to perform.

But this renewal is not about doing or about acquiring knowledge or maintaining control. It is about opening our spirits to the powerful touch of His love. The greater body of ministers in this day need love, too, but the idea of being swept off your feet by Jesus Christ is difficult for many of them to accept. Some even have to force themselves to romance their own wives. But the emotional relationship between husband and wife foreshadows the powerful love relationship between Jesus Christ and His bride. This is not something perverse, but it is pure and holy. Men as well as women need permission to surrender their feelings to the Lord without fear of improper love or even lust. Let go.

One of the most touching testimonies I have heard from the platform in Toronto during my well over 100 plus visits, was from an evangelist from Finland. His wife had suffered terribly with a nine-year battle with brain cancer. During the four years since her death, he had gone everywhere trying to regain his feelings for life and for the Lord. As a last resort, he came to Toronto hoping God would touch him.

That afternoon he had attended the meeting devoted to prayer for ministers and their spouses. For more than four hours this evangelist had remained on the carpet as waves of Jesus' love had swept over him. By the time the evening renewal meeting began, he had to be helped to the platform by two men, one under each arm. He could scarcely talk, so caught up was he in the love of Jesus. As he testified, I doubt there was a dry eye in the room. Tears streamed down my cheeks, too. God came to a man desperate and in need of His love and God met him.

But what if He doesn't touch me?

Fears Of Rejection And Abandonment

If you grew up in church, you may have heard that old hymn, *Pass Me Not, O Gentle Saviour.* Like the blind man crying out by the roadside when Jesus was coming his way, the writer of this hymn wrote it as a plea for a person in need of Jesus' touch. *While on others thou art calling, do not pass me by.* I love that song. But are its implications a real possibility? Would Jesus touch others and not me?

On my arrival in Toronto the first time, I remember thinking, "Oh no, not another meeting where you have to *get* something! For some reason, it is always a challenge for me to receive. No matter how many people who have prayed with me, urging me to "receive," I can't seem to.

In our prayer group in the early '70s when several of us Baptist young women were trying to "receive the baptism in the Holy Spirit," we tried everything- even visiting churches of other denominations. One night as we were standing in a circle in our apartment, with every head bowed and every eye closed, we were asking the Lord to baptize us in the Holy Spirit. We didn't know what to expect so we were listening for the sounds of wind or God to suddenly ignite our feelings. Shortly, our Persian cat made her way down the steps and walked into the middle of the group, her bushy tail brushing our legs. We screamed—but unfortunately not in tongues!

How many thoughts plague us and cause us to feel that we are somehow unpleasing to God, that we are not praying "hard enough," or fasting enough or reading the Bible as we should. Like Adam and Eve hiding from God after they sinned, we are afraid to confront Him for fear He will reject us. But Jesus died and rose again to close that gap. He took the responsibility on Himself to suffer to close that gap. God is in the business of creating in you a desire to do that which is best for you, not handing you a bouquet of "have to's." These often unspoken "rules" have the ability to turn the Good News into Bad News, a new form of slavery to "oughts."

Closely related is the fear that we will be abandoned by God, that He will come and then go because He really didn't like being with us all that much. Do you feel like that? If so, you are not alone, but you are also believing something that is not true. The reason you are here on earth is to be a "container for the Holy Spirit." That is why you are dissatisfied unless you are completely full of the Holy Spirit.

When I finally did receive the baptism in the Holy Spirit, as I shared earlier along with all the other young ladies in our prayer group, there still was a "piece" I missed: the part where the Apostle Paul encouraged the brethren not to be drunk with wine but to be constantly filled with the Holy Spirit. It had never occurred to me that it would be good to ask God to keep me filled. That is the secret of the joyful Christian life. We were designed to have the need of continuous nourishment from Jesus, the True Vine. I had gone for years without any sense of His Presence. It can only be that He never left me. I walked through a desert, and He sustained me.

Perhaps that was the reason for my dryness. When I blurted out my dilemma to Guy Chevreau the first time we received prayer at the pastors' meeting in Toronto, Guy asked what our names were, I said, "We are the Fishes and we are really dry." To which Guy replied, "Well then, let the River flow."

I started weeping. Believe me, crying counts as a "manifestation." It is the beginning of the Lord's process of softening the heart.

Heart Problems

Cynicism is not a characteristic of intelligence but a hardened heart. For years I found it difficult to believe when I saw others professing to be "blessed" at a meeting that it was really happening. Why? Because it was not happening to me. I judged others by my own experience, or lack of it, not realizing that that cynicism was shutting me off from the flow of God.

I also only allowed God to bless me in certain ways. I enjoyed inspiring messages. I loved acquiring information about the Lord and the Christian walk. But I did not go in for the "thrills and chills" and was too proud to think that I needed such experiences. I believed (dry as I was) that I could fulfill my ministry without them. And to worship at the shrine of peripheral experience was to demand something else of God other than what He promised to give in Scripture.

You may be where I was. If so, you are not alone. One of Jesus' twelve disciples fell into this category, too—although the poor guy has been nicknamed by the body of Christ for the only recorded incident in his life in which he displayed doubt. It is possible to label yourself just as blithely as we label Thomas, by characterizing yourself in certain ways: "I'm not one for emotional experiences." "I don't 'go down.'" "I don't think much of all this mum-jumbo." These labels trap you, limiting your realm of experience to what has already happened. Better to say, "I have some questions, but I'm open to whatever God has for me."

But it is hard when you have been excluded from how God seems to be blessing many others.

Thomas was not present the night when Jesus first appeared to the disciples after His resurrection. They had been hovering together, devastated emotionally because their Master had been unjustly and mercilessly killed. One can only imagine the horror of their grief. All their hopes had been disappointed. Three years of their lives had been seemingly wasted. Already they were beginning to doubt what they had seen. One of their number, Mary Magdalene, had even been hallucinating that she had witnessed Him alive!

Suddenly the Lord Jesus Himself came and stood in the room with them, although the door had been shut tight. In wonder and amazement they watched as He showed them His hands and His side. The very sight of Jesus filled them with gladness and joy, but Jesus had more for them. He pronounced blessing upon them: "Peace be to you! As the Father has sent Me, I also send you." (John 20:21, NKJV) Then He breathed on them the powerful breath of spiritual life and said, "Receive the Holy Spirit." (V 22). The next breath everyone in the room drew was filled with the life-giving presence of the Holy Spirit, the very breath of God. Finally, Jesus imparted to them the authority to forgive —one of the most powerful ministries anyone can have because it opens the Kingdom of heaven and every work of grace to the undeserving.

One can only imagine the awe of those moments the resurrected Lord had with His disciples. It was a powerful visitation that brought a restoration of hope, vision, release from sorrow, commission, impartation, blessing and gladness. Unfortunately Thomas missed it. (Be careful not to miss fellowship these days for frivolous reasons.)

If the disciples were anything like us, by the following day they had probably condensed the entire experience into a formula for "receiving." When they found Thomas and told him about their night, I wonder if they even tried to "breathe" on Thomas taking advantage of their new impartation and blow upon him the same blessing? Or if he received nothing, did they exercise their newfound ministry of forgiveness and ask him if there were any in his past he needed to forgive?

But Thomas was angry, still suffering the grief of having lost Jesus and feeling he had now been passed by. You can almost hear the thoughts running through his mind: *Why did Jesus wait until a moment when I wasn't there to bless everyone else? What did I do wrong? Did I offend Him in some way? Does he consider me in the same category as Judas? Perhaps that's the only time He'll appear and I missed it. I'm left alone while all the others got special treatment.*

No wonder Thomas blurted out, "Unless I see in His hands the print of the nails, and put my finger into the print of the nails, and put my hand into His side, I will not believe." (John 20:25 NKJV) He was almost daring God to do something special for him. After all, didn't his years of faithfulness warrant the same attention from Jesus that everyone else had received?

But seven days passed, and Jesus did not reappear. Then, on the eighth day, as the doors were shut again and they were all together, He came again, for Thomas' sake. As though He had been standing there during Thomas' outburst, Jesus answered the disciple's challenge: "Reach your finger here, and look at My hands; and reach your hand here, and put it into My side. Do not be unbelieving, but believing." (Verse 27, NKJV)

Jesus allowed Thomas to experience Him in a way that others had not. Jesus permitted him to not only see Him but to touch Him exactly as Thomas demanded. According to what Jesus told him, I believe he received the ability, through this experience with the Lord, to have great faith.

But lest we ever get proud of some spiritual experience of our own, we must remember what Jesus told Thomas and the rest of the disciples: "Because you have seen Me, you have believed. Blessed are those who have not seen and yet have be-lieved." (Verse 29 NKJV)

Have you ever noticed that the other disciples did not believe until they saw Jesus, either? We receive a visitation from the Lord not because we are more spiritual than others but because we are needy. It is the acknowledgment of deep need that causes us to hunger after Him until we receive.

How Can Doubters Receive?

Thomas may have assumed mistakenly that because he had not been present when the others saw Jesus, that he would never be able to see Him himself. When others seem to be receiving from the Lord, never think —because you have not been blessed as they have—that the Lord doesn't want to bless you, too. Some of our brothers and sisters give up on seeking anything God has for them because they start to assume that because they sought a little while and did not receive anything, that these gifts and blessings were not for them. But this was not true for Thomas. Not only did the Lord want Thomas to see Him, but because the disciple asked for more, he was permitted more.

Many in the visitation have been asking, "More, Lord, for me!"

Assuming that you are some special case—that you are so different or unworthy that you cannot have the same blessings as others—is a subtle form of pride that sets us a roadblock be-tween you and the Lord. As long as you think that He does not want a particular blessing or gift for you and you do not ask, you may be deceived out of having it. Believing a lie is the way to be deceived.

Remember that your difficulty in receiving is a challenge from the Lord to keep you seeking. This is what Jesus meant when in the story about the woman who would not give up praying or in the verse, "Blessed are those which do hunger and thirst after righteousness; for they shall be filled." (Matthew 5:6 KJV) or "[Keep] asking, [keep] seeking and [keep] knocking for the door shall be opened unto you..."(Matthew 7: 7-12 and Luke

11:11-13) The truly hungry keep asking, keep seeking and keep knocking.

Thomas' false assumptions erupted from a grieved, disappointed heart. Anger is a stage of grief, and Thomas was clearly there when he first heard that Jesus was alive. So were the other disciples whom Mary Magdalene told she had seen the Lord. Mary, the first human being to see Jesus alive and touch Him, had encountered Him when lingering near the tomb. Her heart's desire was met beyond her wildest expectations.

But is it possible to be brought so low by anger over griefs, hurts, offenses and disillusionment with trials we have faced that we become not only skeptical but cynical. Cynicism lay behind Thomas' angry outburst. Probably he did not expect to be visited personally by Jesus. Almost sarcastically he dared the other disciples to keep believing, and he implied that unless he, too, received an unlikely rare appearance, he would not be as gullible as they were. He did not say, "I cannot believe." He said, "I will not."

I can identify with such doubt. It is difficult to watch other Christians having wonderful experiences and not be a little jealous. Sometimes the Lord provokes people to "a godly jealousy"of this kind so they will keep seeking until He answers, "Ask and it shall be given you, and you shall find, knock and the door shall be opened unto you."(Matthew 7:7) Each of these verb forms in Greek implies continuously asking, seeking and knocking. To continue knocking means that for awhile the door stays closed. Ask yourself, How badly do I want God? to what lengths will I go in order to find Him?

As I have sought prayer repeatedly, the Lord has graciously rinsed cynicism out of my life. I find it much easier to believe now when others tell me of their experiences. I am also learning to pay attention to mental impressions and pictures I used to ignore, thinking they were only me.

In all the mistakes I made in my dry season, I kept hanging around. That is what Thomas did. Even though he was angry, cynical and jealous, he kept hanging out with the guys. Maybe he did not know what else to do. But he did not give up. He was right where he should be when Jesus visited again.

Do not let discouragement drive you away from the Church. That is where Jesus lives—in His body and where He shows up in every season of refreshing. He will never forsake her. And no matter how downcast you may be, He will not forsake you, either. Many Christians are in for a glorious visitation simply because they keep hanging around waiting for God to meet them.

When Jesus finally visited again, He told Thomas what to do in order to receive from Him. Thomas needed the faith that would come from touching Jesus. When Jesus told him to touch His wounds, I am sure Thomas obeyed. And as he did, something happened to him, for he exclaimed, "My Lord and my God!" (John 20:28). The exclamation point reveals his surprise and awe. He could not help but worship Jesus.

Once we know that what is happening to other people is real, we must do everything possible to obey the Lord ourselves. Whatever Jesus wants you to do, in order to best receive from Him, do it, - even if you risk making a mistake.

But how do I receive from the Lord?

7 - RECEIVING GOD'S TOUCH

So how can I receive from the Lord? What is the secret of submission to and receiving from Him?

Humble Yourself

We could have gone on awhile without mentioning humility, couldn't we? One of the great stumbling blocks to receiving from God is a proud human spirit: "God resists the proud, but gives grace to the humble." (James 4:6, NKJV) One way to exhibit pride is when we are choosy about where we will go in order to receive, or about who prays for us, or about what manifestations we are willing to receive. Pride is lurking when we are unwilling to forgive others for offenses. There are other ways, too, in which pride leaks out—such as loving our dignity more than we love Jesus.

Surrender yourself completely to the Lord. Do not think He has nothing for you because you are too wicked—or, on the other hand, too mature in the Spirit. Regardless of how vile we have been, our only prayer is to touch the Lord and be filled with His righteousness. Regardless of how mature we are, we can always come to know Him better.

Surrender yourself to God from your heart, body, soul and spirit. Tell Him you are willing to allow Him to do with you as He sees fit. This amounts to surrendering yourself anew to the Lordship of Jesus Christ.

Give Up Your Agenda

When Jesus said, "No one can be My disciple who does not give up His own possessions, He also meant anything, including your own agenda. Your way and His way are very likely two different things. You are learning His way as His disciple. Our own agendas are stumbling blocks to His ways.

Before God saves Aunt Petunia and Uncle Fred, or answers the other requests on your prayer list, He wants to touch you. Perhaps you are on someone else's prayer list and what is about to happen to you is an answer to their prayers. Before Jesus heals your body, He may want to touch some heart issues first. Without realizing it, you may be attempting to confine the Lord by defining for Him the process by which He should do so.

When seeking the Lord, surrender your agenda to Him. This gives Him the freedom to touch you in the way He chooses. It also opens your heart to the unexpected and puts you in awe of the God who can do anything—and probably will!

Forgive and ask His forgiveness for any hardness of heart and any judgments you have made against others. When you judge others, you are actually judging yourself, too. I was sharing at a meeting one night when a woman approached me who was having difficulty receiving prayer at the altar. She said she felt like something was blocking her. It occurred to me, perhaps by word of knowledge, to ask her if she had been one who had judged the participation of others in the renewal blessings by thinking they were going too far and making spectacles of themselves. She admitted that she had. When she asked the Lord to forgive her, she immediately collapsed to the floor and began laughing with joy. She no longer cared because the fullness of the Spirit was overwhelming her.

Any time there is an attitude we hold onto that conflicts with the Holy Spirit's love, let it go. It's not worth the terrible cost of blocking the Holy Spirit's flow into and through your life.

Be As Dependent As A Child

Receiving is more than presenting yourself for prayer. It is more than "going down under the power." Even this will become an empty ritual unless you open your spirit to the Lord each time in childlike trust and dependency. Remember this: It is not about falling nor any other outward sign; it is about 'falling in love' with Jesus.

Childlikeness is not the childishness of immaturity. It embraces all the positive characteristics children possess: wonder, simplicity, playfulness, trust, naive innocence about evil, lack of inhibition, quick recovery from anger. Childlikeness causes us to acknowledge our dependence on the power of the Holy Spirit, and not on our human strength or cleverness, to meet the challenges the enemy presents.

Surrender like a helpless child to the loving arms of your Heavenly Father—even if you are 95 years old!—and let Him love you. Don't try to analyze your problems and work them out on your own. The powerful reality of Sabbath rest is promised to believers who cease striving in their own strength and allow themselves to be touched by His overwhelming love. The same childlike surrender that motivates you to risk jumping in to the river in the first place will help you to continue receiving blessing after blessing from Him.

John Carr, a pastor from Dundee, Scotland, is in heaven now. But he ministered several times in our congregation. His mentors had been prominent people in the Welsh Revival. The Lord used John to resolve many problems in local churches. I remember asking him how he managed to do this and remain personally encouraged. His reply, "I'm only Father's little child," he said. "He gives me the grace to do it." Isn't that the key to the Kingdom of Heaven that Jesus spoke of?

Receive The Filling Of The Holy Spirit

Set your mind on loving God. Relax. Don't try to strain for a blessing. Rather, accept it as a gift He gives you eagerly. What you are asking Him for is to be filled with the Holy Spirit today. You may have asked to be filled with the Holy Spirit years ago, or you may believe you received the Holy spirit at conversion. In either case, ask Him for more of His Spirit, for all the fullness of God.

God will answer this prayer because He wants you to know His love and the power of His Presence more than you can imagine. He gave His only begotten Son so that you might have the fullness of His Spirit. And God knows that the receiving the work of the Holy Spirit is your only hope for the changes you long for.

Yield

After a few moments, as you wait in His presence, you may feel nothing, or you may begin to experience some physical manifestation. You may continue to wait on Him quietly, or you may find yourself wanting to dance, leap, shout or roar. Or you may sense an internal urge to praise God in a language you have never learned. Open your mouth and try, even if it seems strange. Don't be afraid, God knows your heart, and He will extend His arms to you as you run toward Him.

Yielding to any God-given manifestation increases the sense of His presence; but suppressing it will quench the Spirit.

How Much Is Too Much?

Every few months during the renewal and at any other time, I have read articles by well-meaning Christians cautioning the Body of Christ about what they consider "too many" manifestations or "too much" prayer. They seem to want everyone to stop receiving at the point they deem appropriate, as though we need to get up now and get on with Kingdom business.

But why? We have been attempting Kingdom business for years without His fullness and His power. Perhaps these fellow believers fear that believers will seek the emotion of being filled with the Holy Spirit without allowing the Spirit access to their character. To that I heard the Lord say to me:

"There Are No Toxic Levels Of The Holy Spirit!"

Character influenced by the fruit of the Holy Spirit is vital. And without love, all the gifts and manifestations are as a "noisy gong or a clanging cymbal." (I Corinthians 13:1) But who is to say when we have had enough and have become over saturated with the presence of God: How much of Him is "too much"? Is there such a thing as "too much love, joy, peace fullness, too many gifts of the Spirit or empowering for service? Why do we think we can ever imbibe all there is of our eternal Heavenly Father? Why can't we allow the Lord to manage the dispensing of His Holy Spirit?

Once again I say that both Jesus and later the Apostle Paul taught us to "keep asking, keep seeking and keep knocking"—the literal Greek translation of Luke 11:9.

So long as the Holy Spirit is blessing you as you receive prayer, continue receiving and experiencing. As you are filled daily with the spirit, you will notice that as you give out, you need to be refilled again and again. But as you keep your focus on receiving the love of Jesus and desiring to bless Him with your submission and faithfulness, you need not worry about receiving too much! There is no such thing.

So, as my husband, Bill, prays often, "Keep coming, Holy Spirit! And if in either word or deed we tell you are unwelcome, come anyway! We need you!"

As I continued to receive touch after touch from the Holy Spirit, the Lord touched me in a more powerful way than I have ever experienced in my life. This is what happened.

8 - SEEING HIM

"...and he endured seeing Him who was
unseen."(Hebrews 11:27)

For part of the time Bill went to seminary in Fort Worth, I worked as the secretary-receptionist at the General Portland Cement Plant on the north side of "Cowtown." I was the only woman on site, the lone rose among thorns. After I had worked there for several months, processing mail and purchase orders and handling and relating phone calls to various areas of the plant, they gave me a plant tour. I donned my hard hat and safety shoes and climbed into the front seat of one of the company pick-ups. The office manager and general foreman drove me to every site of plant operation—an experience that put faces to the voices I had talked to for months on the phone, from the quarry to the loading dock, and gave me a vision for the small part I played in the production of cement.

The center of the plant operation was the kiln—a pipe more than 25 yards in length and several feet in diameter. The key to production: keeping the temperature hot enough to process the limestone from the quarry into a component that could be made into powdered cement. The kiln rotated slowly day and night, monitored constantly by three shifts of laborers who did nothing but make certain there was enough natural gas feeding the furnace to keep the fire inside hotter than three thousand degrees Fahrenheit.

From a small, heat shielded window, I looked inside and caught a glimpse of the fire that made my own job necessary. If the temperature cooled only slightly, the quality of the cement would be diminished. So the jobs of hundreds of laborers, as well as those of the corporate heads in Dallas, depended on whether the fire in the kiln kept glowing white-hot.

This helps me understand now why I must stay on fire for Jesus. All our works, as we pass from this earthly life into His Presence, will face the test of fire. Every task we perform strictly out of duty or impure motives, rather than passion for Him, will be burned up as wood, hay or stubble. Every product of our lives —the words we have spoken, the deeds we have done—must be able to survive this fire.

Human beings, trained to judge according to the world's value system, are incapable of testing the spiritual quality of anyone's work. So in the eternity, some deeds will be rewarded that on earth were cursed. Others will be consumed that on earth were "blessed."

The key for us is not to perfect the products of our lives, but to make sure our hearts burn white-hot with love for Jesus. God has never looked for workers but worshippers. This is what Jesus told the woman at the well of Samaria: "An hour is coming, and now is, when true worshippers shall worship the Father in spirit and truth; for such people the Father seeks to be His worshippers." (John 4:23) Those whose hearts are on fire with love for Jesus will produce eternal works in the Kingdom of God.

But this is possible only if the Lord mercifully touches and fills us with His Spirit. The Holy Spirit prepares us for our ultimate union with Christ when we see Him face to face. He also ushers us into dimensions of God's presence now, preparing our spirits with a priceless sense of His fullness so that we (as Paul prayed),

> ...being rooted and grounded in love, may be able to comprehend with all the saints what is the breadth and length and height and depth, and to know the love of Christ which surpasses knowledge that you may be filled up to all the fullness of God. (Ephesians 3:17-19)

The ability to stay on fire for Jesus is also a work of grace, then initiated by Him. All we need to do is respond.

Firing Our Passion

As you examine the pages of Scripture, you notice that the lives of those God uses follow a similar pattern. The spiritual journey to find God and be used by Him includes a period of unconcern in which the person is content without knowing God (though he may wonder about Him or even be fascinated by Him). Then comes the sudden intrusion of God into his circumstances - a burning bush, a visitation by an angel, and encounter with ultimate reality. Afterward the individual is tested in a dry wilderness experience, sometimes for years. Then, about the time he has given up all hope, he is once again confronted by God (just as suddenly as he was overtaken by the wilderness) and led into the true purpose for his life.

Abraham, Joseph, Moses, all the prophets, the disciples of Jesus, Saul of Tarsus, even the Son of God Himself, made this journey. Nor has God abandoned this pathway in our generation, when values and expectations created in us the false hope that He will choose a shorter route.

Sometimes it seems that successful brothers and sisters have taken a shortcut around this process. But as we look more closely, we see that the proof is not in the fruit of their lives, but in the depth of their knowledge and love of Christ. Every vision that will survive His fire has been birthed in the fire, tried by the flames, passed through death and into resurrection, where not even the forces of hell can destroy it.

So what is the purpose of revival? For the Lord to draw near to bless and refresh His Church; when the Bridegroom initiates, through overtures of love and blessing, a season of making Himself known to His people and firing their passion for Him.

Because we are incapable of generating passion for God on our own, apart from the fire of His Spirit, it is imperative that we not miss the day when the Holy Spirit reveals Himself. To reject His overtures grieves Him, quenches our passion for Jesus, diminishes the quality of our work and leaves us living life at the meager level of inadequate knowledge of His love.

Regaining Our First Love

The Lord is flooding all who are open to Him with a ravishing sense of His passionate love for His bride. Of all the gifts, this is (as I have said) the most precious to me. I consider myself a love-hungry person before God. I am willing now to receive anything—laughter to the point of drunkenness, shaking, trembling, roaring, dancing, jumping, convulsing, jerking, anything that that is not illegal, immoral, fattening or heretical—if I think for one brief instant that such antics will accompany a tiny taste of His love for me.

Why? Because I have lived too long without it.

I have already recounted how the fullness of the Spirit that the apostle Paul talked about in Ephesians 3—so glorious that he reached for the strongest adjectives to try to describe it - drained from me long ago. I comforted myself with the thought that I must be faithful to my posts even if it meant I never felt anything again. My work itself, I assumed, was a manifestation of my love for Jesus.

I did not realize that I belonged, instead, to the Ephesian church Jesus addressed in Revelation 2:4: "I have this against you, that you have left your first love." This was the church that thought the Lord prized productivity and visible results above passion for Jesus. They were desperately wrong. No amount of preaching, teaching, witnessing, praying, fasting, serving, discerning, book-writing, pod-casting, blogging or church planting will ever be enough to fill His heart in the absence of your love. So far as Jesus is concerned, doing everything right with an empty heart is not to have done anything at all. He warns those content in this state that their lamp stand will be removed.

The lamp stand in the Tabernacle of Moses, and later in the Temple of Solomon, was not a set of wax candles that burned themselves out of existence. It was a hollow, decorative lamp from which twelve stems were connected to a single, vertical pipe, much like a trained vine with branches. Oil poured into the central pipe flowed into the stems as well, filling them up. Each stem contained a wick that burned when ignited with a bright light that illuminated the service going on in the Holy Place of the Temple. The oil symbolizes the fullness of the Spirit, which alone is the fuel for the Light that brightens our own lives and service for Him. Without abiding in the source of oil, we are working in the dark.

I had been working in the dark for some years. There was a big gap, I realized, between where I was and where I wanted to be. But I could not figure out how to get back into the light. I could "remember...from where you have fallen" (Revelation 2:5), but I had no idea how to repent, to go back 180 degrees and re-cover my first love for Jesus.

If everything we have from God—even repentance, the ability to turn—is given because of His grace, I needed desperately for God to grant me the ability to recover my passion for Him. But the years wore on without it. I resembled many Christians going through religious motions and attempting to maintain some semblance of enthusiasm so as not to discourage others (even though my inner feelings would slip out to those who knew me well).

What I did not realize was that the Holy Spirit had been doing an inner healing work for years that would prepare me to both receive and contain the blessing of a new move of the Holy Spirit in my own heart.

Ruth's Journey Into Blessing

The tragedies of life had all but destroyed Ruth, a foreigner to Israel. Her husband had died and she was penniless and barren. It would be difficult to find another husband since her association with the Israelites had isolated her socially in Moab, a country cursed by the God of Israel. Ruth had only one rela-tionship left—with her mother-in-law, Naomi, whom she loved. Together they made their way back to Bethlehem.

Naomi believed that she had been cursed and said so five times in the first chapter of Ruth. She had lost her husband and two sons and now she believed she had fallen out of favor with God. "I went out full," she said, "but the Lord has brought me back empty." (Ruth 1:21)

The wilderness produces those feelings of devastation. Believers who have endured a wilderness experience have likely seen all hell unleashed against them. They may have been tested to the limits of human endurance through repeated heartache and disappointment, and may have even encountered the last enemy, death. Maybe they have seen others all around them blessed, while a cloud of doom seems to hover over their own heads. Maybe they have suffered the mental anguish of misunderstanding from the Body of Christ. Perhaps they have given up and, like Naomi, feel isolated from God.

As Ruth and Naomi returned to Israel, Ruth went out to find grain for their sustenance. She "happened" into the field of Boaz, a wealthy landowner who turned out to be one of their nearest relatives, one who held the potential of removing her shame and transforming her future into great blessing. Boaz was kind and protective, making sure Ruth got extra grain as she gleaned behind his crew. You can tell, reading between the lines, that Boaz' esteem and affection for her increased with every encounter, although his pure heart would not allow him to think she might find him attractive.

The turning point of the story finds her having done all she could do, lying exhausted at the feet of Boaz, waiting for him to awaken from sleep and redeem her. Refreshing lay ahead.

This is where many in the Church are today. The season of dryness has brought us to a place of devastation, fruitlessness, utter dependence on the Lord Jesus Christ. Thank God for the wilderness that has led so many of His people to the painful revelation that only in lack and hunger for Him will we see His provision. During a day of visitation, we see that it is "not by might nor by power, but by My Spirit." (Zechariah 4:6)

Jesus promised in the Sermon on the Mount that the following people will be blessed: those who are poor in spirit, reduced to mourning, hungry and thirsty for Him, meek, persecuted for righteousness. But the blessing will not take the outward fruit of divine favor before they come into an intimate knowledge of the Lord that will fulfill His promise of a New Covenant: "They shall all know Me, from the least of them to the greatest of them." (Jeremiah 31:34)

A day is coming when the intimate knowledge of God, made possible only by the passion ignited by the Holy Spirit, will be experienced not by a few mystics whose books are lost on the back shelves of theological libraries, but by the least of the saints who will find themselves caught up in fellowship with the Lord. Then we will understand that all favor from God comes not because we have earned it through our faithfulness, but by His grace alone. He has had designs on us since the moment He saw us.

So everyone who is seeking Jesus Christ-ministers of large congregations, pastors of tiny congregations, believers who have survived every imaginable tragedy or who are simply aware that something is missing and long to be refreshed—are like Ruth, seeking refuge in the God who loves them and has a covenant with them to restore them and be their Husband. If you are reading this fifty years from now, I want you to understand that you must not live without an intimate communion with the Lord that is ignited in times of visitation "while He may be found." (Isaiah 55:6)

And if someone we know longs for the fire of passion that can be transmitted only by a fresh touch from the Holy Spirit, it is wrong for us to dishonor such desperation by claiming that he or she simply wants to experience a manifestation. Desperate believers are too devastated to believe that a simple thrill or even a whiff of inspiration will restore them. They are seeking the loving touch of the only One who matters.

Nor will the Lord allow them to be disappointed.

My Immersion In God's Love

Since I first witnessed a supernatural visitation of God in the early '70's in Dallas, TX, I realize it is possible for unbelievers to be in a room in which they feel God's awesome presence and where they cannot help but give themselves to Him. I understand from reports of the Welsh revival of 1904 that fishermen out at sea were drawn to shore and into meetings where they met Jesus Christ. Accounts of the Azusa Street revival a year or two later report (as I mentioned earlier) that God "blocked off" an area surrounding the old mission building with His presence. Anyone who happened into that radius of several blocks was drawn into the meetings and into a relationship with Him. People from all over the world longing for a touch from God were drawn to that place of outpouring in Los Angeles.

Although I have seen many evidences of His grace and blessing since that time in Dallas, I have seen no other corporate visitation like it. Everything else has contained elements of human effort. This current visitation, from my observation, is the first refreshing in all that time that has not had "manmade" stamped all over it. It is, I believe the refreshing of the saints that Jonathan Edwards spoke of that is the first phase of revival that precedes the salvation of sinners.

But the blessings of this phase cannot be bypassed. It is the stage in which the fires of passion for Jesus will be ignited that will burn in believers' hearts and cause the works of their hands in the coming decades to survive the fire of testing.

Five months after the current visitation began for me, I had been touched several times by the Holy Spirit's power when I had an experience that I have been able to talk about little but which has had life-changing ramifications.

I had traveled to eastern Maryland to speak at a women's retreat. It was a weekend of great blessing. After the meetings were over, I was eating in the cafeteria when a lovely woman named Carolyn Jones, a member of the West Baltimore chapter of Women's Aglow, came up to the table. She was weeping and wanted to express her gratitude to me for encouraging her to be herself in the presence of the Lord. She asked me if she could hug me. I stood up and wrapped my arms around her.

Instantly the power of the Holy Spirit fell on me. I began to laugh and cry at the same moment, from the depths of my inner being, I began to make a noise that sounded like a wail. I began to tremble and almost collapsed. Two women at the table supported me, one under each arm, helping me out of the dining room and down the hall to my room. They laid me down on the bed and remained with me.

At that moment, suddenly I felt as though I were being vacuumed up with powerful force into a realm I had never been in during all my years of being a Christian. I could not see Him, but I could feel His closeness as though nothing stood between us. I felt that for my entire life I had been worshipping Him behind a wall, and that the wall had suddenly fallen down to reveal Him to me.

Waves of indescribable love washed over me. I understood in that moment that God had been drawing me from the beginning of my life. He is so awesome in His glory, and so magnetic in His presence, that worship was being pulled from me by a force greater than myself. But it was the force of magnificent love. I had always read in the Bible, and believed, that God is love. But now I was experiencing it.

The reason that the Bible says simply, "God is love," is that no superlative in any human language can describe the all-consuming love of Jesus for your soul. Suddenly I knew why Jesus died for me. His love was so great that He was driven by love to the cross, so that I and others could be with Him forever.

And suddenly I understood Paul's statement "that at the name of Jesus every knee should bow...and every tongue should confess that Jesus Christ is Lord." (Philippians 2:10-11) You could not possibly stand in the presence of the risen Lord, over even by an act of choice decide to kneel or to fall on your face. Your human body has no choice but, in the sheer power of His presence, to collapse at His feet. John, on the Isle of Patmos, fell as one dead because He experienced such an encounter.

"No man," God told Moses, "can see Me and live!" (Exodus 33:20) I had always imagined that this meant that I would be afraid of God. But now, as I lay on that bed after the retreat, the force of His love was so powerful that I wanted to die and be with Him. I realized as it says in I Corinthians 15:53, "This mortal must put on immortality." I have no way of taking in the love of Jesus, and of being able to reciprocate this love in my physical body.

Oh the horror of Judgment Day, when those who have spurned the love of Jesus will be confronted with the full force of their decision, with no hope of ever seeing Him again! The agony of seeing Jesus and then to be deprived of Him for eternity would be the ultimate torment. And to know forever that all your sin could have been erased by His blood, burned away by one word from your mouth acknowledging His Lordship, would be hell itself.

That morning at the women's retreat, I had preached a message about the woman who invaded the Pharisee's home and anointed Jesus' feet. Our only hope of becoming pure, I had told the women, is being in His cleansing presence. We should never turn away from Him, but understand how much our worship means to Him.

Before this I had imagined that Jesus would stare straight ahead stoically while the myriad of believers worshipped Him from a distance. I knew now that He was visibly affected, even melted, by the small words and phrases spoken to Him. He lived to hear me worship Him; He died for the privilege of hearing it! I could sense His glorious pleasure at the sound of my voice, at every cry from my lips—"Lord Jesus! Lord Jesus!" for that was all I could say.

"When He appears," wrote the apostle John, "we shall be like Him, because we shall see Him just as He is." (I John 3:2) The brief moments I spent in His manifest presence adjusted my thinking. All the pursuits of life were nothing. All the earthly possessions that I ever thought important disappeared into oblivion. I kept thinking, It's all Jesus! There is nothing but Jesus! Nothing in life mattered anymore except being in that place. I wanted to die, the pleasure of being near Him was so great.

The women from the retreat who had remained in the room were worshipping along with me. I wanted to urge them to continue in worship because I could sense His magnificent love for them and the great pleasure their words brought the Lord. "If only you could understand how much He longs for and loves your worship," I wanted to tell them. But I could say nothing but "Lord Jesus!" over and over.

In His presence I saw that each of us has one problem only: that we do not know how much Jesus loves us. If we did, we would do nothing to grieve Him. As I realized how important each of us is to Him, and how dearly passionately He loves us, there was no jealousy in it, for I could feel His love for me as well. Gathering people into the arms of Jesus, I thought, is the only pursuit of eternal value. That's all that is important to Him.

The scriptures were passing through me at "lightning" speed. No one should doubt that the scriptures are divinely inspired. I have been in the presence of the One who wrote them. He is truly the Word of God. The phrase the way into the holiest kept echoing in my mind. I knew I was in the holiest—in a dimension of God's presence that had been concealed from me. But I had done nothing to gain entry. It was all grace. I had been neither fasting nor praying. And now I was aware that He not only approved of me, but desired to pour His love upon me as I was—His love that was pure, clean, holy and completely trustworthy.

When I awoke from this realm, the glory of it gradually fading, I said, "I will serve Him as long as I live. Nothing will keep me from Him. I only want to immerse myself in the luxury of pleasing Him."

In the years since, I have been deeply affected by those moments of powerfully sensing His love. In fact, I can think of little else. I remember it every day. My faith is rock-hard in the wonderful presence of the Lord Jesus that awaits me. It is difficult to think that I may live for forty or more years until I can see Him again. But rather than dread the moment, I anticipate it.

None of what I experienced was in the realm of imagination. If it were, I could reimagine it. Nor do I find it easy to speak of the experience. I have spoken of it rarely because it was the most sacred moment of my life. The few times I have attempted to describe it to anyone, even Bill, I could not look at the people I was talking to.

But my life has been different. I continue to live in the awe of the love I experienced. And my desire for one more tiny glimpse of Him motivates me to give my life for Him.

Where does renewal go, you ask me?

To the bosom of Jesus. Do not let anything stop you, because one moment in His presence is worth a lifetime of heartache and desperate searching. To know we will spend eternity in the presence of His great love is an incomparable treasure.

He initiated this renewal; we did not. He is reviving our passion for Him so that we may bring pleasure to His heart and begin to feel His love—perhaps for the first time. How far away I had fallen from it, yet how little I had ever known of it! Not if I spent a lifetime sitting and worshipping Him all day long would I ever be able to do justice to His glory and return to Him the power of His great love. The love of Jesus is no longer a concept to me. He is more real than the reality I see around me.

For those who have never experienced anything like this, yet serve Him by faith, I have the highest respect. "Blessed are they who did not see," Jesus told Thomas, "and yet have believed." (John 20:29) Perhaps a reward awaits others that may no longer be mine because I have caught a glimpse of Him. However, all this was by grace. I did nothing to cause it or "earn" it. God, the Father, allowed me to "see" His Son, the object of His affection so that I might better comprehend His love.

Someone said to me soon after the experience, "Now you will see more." My only thought was, What else is there to see? I care nothing about visions of principalities or illuminations of heavenly scenes or what someone has called "mapping the throne room of heaven." All I want is more of Him. He is everything.

Are You Afraid Of Intimacy?

The night before this life-changing encounter, as I lay my head on the pillow, my thoughts turned to the Lord. I fact, I felt a sense of His love begin to ravish my heart. I had not felt any such thing for nearly eighteen years. But I had become so full of the Holy Spirit, soaking in His presence during the renewal, that I determined to abandon myself to Him and allow Him to take my worship to a new dimension. Now I had the sense that I had deprived myself for many years, through fear, of the joy of knowing Him, and that I would put Him off no longer. So I began to move past the barrier.

Let me travel back to my childhood for a moment. During my childhood, I was molested repeatedly by a neighbor. Since then, and weakened through seasons of low self-worth, I had been afraid of certain dimensions of intimacy out of a sense of shame. My ability to communicate my love for Jesus in worship, for example, had been severely inhibited. I relied on singing, but even singing could not break through the wall that had stood between me and Jesus. I spent worship times at church keeping track of the time, enjoying and being inspired by the music but never transcending the emotional barrier that would allow me the privilege of expressing the depth of my love for Jesus.

A few times over the years, the Holy Spirit had moved upon me, stirring my passion for Jesus, but I was afraid of strong feelings and wondered, since few people ever spoke of them, whether they were even right. Embarrassed by such depth of feeling, I hid myself from God, afraid to let my feelings go since I did not know where they would lead.

But within moments of my revelation of God's love at the

women's retreat, I found the ability to express my love to Jesus in a more intimate way. Now I understood how much He longed for my fellowship, and how my silence towards Him had robbed Him of pleasure. Now I wanted to do nothing but find words to describe how I felt about Him.

Music, I learned, is only one form of worship and only one means of facilitating intimacy with the Lord. He needs to hear words from our lips—words from our hearts and minds—that express how dear He is to us. It is this form of worship that affords Him the highest pleasure.

Now, my insecurities and fears have diminished, but they have not all disappeared. But understanding the power of His magnificent love makes it easier for me to set aside shortcomings and failures, realizing these are burned away in His awesome presence. Jesus' death on the cross removed the barrier of sin because He will allow nothing to stand between us and the mutual enjoyment of our love for one another. My shyness in His presence is lessening. I am beginning to trust Him with the depths of my emotion, knowing He will never reject me.

Expressing Your Love

Perhaps you, like me, have difficulty allowing yourself to worship God beyond a certain point. Perhaps you are afraid of emotion and find yourself quenching expressions of your love. Remember, His magnificent love is the antithesis of rejection. To feel rejected is to be deceived. All the depth of emotion He created in you is for loving Him deeply, and for loving others in such a way as to draw them into His arms.

Steve Long, a lead pastor of what is now Catch the Fire, made a comment to me about intimate communion with the Lord and how God helped him remove a significant hindrance to him being able to hear from God. "I realized," he said, "that I had been listening to the wrong voice."

Many of the Lord's servants as well have been listening to the voice of their own wounded souls, or the voice of the enemy condemning them for failure, causing them to feel separated from the Lord, or that they are somehow not spiritual enough, or so full of shortcomings that He cannot love them. How tragic!

Jesus accepted the expressions of deeply felt love from the prostitute who crashed the Pharisee's banquet. Her demonstration of affection for Him embarrassed the legalists at the table who believed God's love was based on performance. But Jesus was pleased with and received her worship, forgave her sin and lifted her act of affection as a model of worship for all time. One moment in the Master's presence was enough to cleanse her from a lifetime of adultery. Such is the cleansing power of His presence!

When Paul said that "nothing shall be able to separate us from the love of God, which is in Christ Jesus our Lord" (Romans 8:39), he spoke not about an abstract concept of God's love, or the hope of it, but the knowledge of what it is like in His actual presence.

If you have difficulty overcoming the fear of intimacy, continue to receive prayer. You need to experience God's presence over and over until you stop being afraid of being rejected by Him and until your emotions are released to serve the Highest purpose for which they were created: showering affection on Jesus, and loving your Heavenly Father deeply.

As you are filled with the Holy Spirit, one evidence will be a heart so full of love for the Lord that you want to sing! "[Speak] to one another in psalms and hymns and spiritual songs," admonished Paul, "singing and making melody with your heart to the Lord." (Ephesians 5:19). I have awakened some mornings realizing that my heart has been singing to the Lord while I was asleep. The Lord's voice is drifting through my now-conscious mind, and I am edified as I wake up.

As you sing in your heart to the Lord, the fullness of His Spirit becomes greater in you. Continue to allow the Holy Spirit to fill you, because He will give you words of praise and adoration that please God.

One day as I was searching for words, I heard the Lord say to me, Speak to Me in tongues. I realized then the value of this gift in expressing intimate worship to the Lord.

Peter Lyne, a leader with an international ministry who now lives in New Zealand, received the gift of tongues in 1965 after a time of fervent searching; but when He finally received it, he did not allow it to develop and it gradually fell into disuse. He said it was though he had been given a new suit—excited to wear it on the first day, but taken for granted as time went on. Then the Lord impressed Peter with a challenge: I've given you something very precious. Now what are you going to do with it?

So in the coming weeks, he set aside at least fifteen or twenty minutes every day just to pray in tongues. Within days the gift moved to a new depth. He began to experience a deeper sense of the prophetic words. Interpretation began to flow.

His advice to Christians experiencing the blessings of renewal today: Ask the Lord to take you to new depths.

Developing Intimacy

The revelation of Jesus' love is like that. As we spend time alone with Him in worship, intimacy with Him will develop. Begin to read and meditate on every passage in the Scripture that talks about His love. The mystery of the Song of Solomon is the revelation of the love of Jesus Christ for every member of His Body. In 1 Corinthians 13, Paul is adoring God's love. Try reading that chapter aloud to God and saying, "If I speak with the tongues of me and of angels, and do not have Your love, I have become a noisy gong or a clanging cymbal"—on throughout the entire chapter.

As you examine these and every portion of Scripture, see them as personal communications of His love for you-not merely for everyone in the world, but for you. Do not allow Bible study to be simply a pursuit of the intellect, but receive the words of Scripture as His tender expressions of love.

Allow yourself times when you draw aside in response to the stirring of His love in your heart. I have learned not simply to acknowledge these moments, but to stop what I am doing and turn aside to be alone with Him. In these moments, allow yourself the luxury of drinking in His presence, being filled again and again with His love. Learn to remain there as long as you sense that you need to. This is how you keep your passion for Jesus burning with the white-hot fire that tests works of true spiritual value. Such passion burns away impure motives and causes you to do whatever you do out of love for Him.

As you are overshadowed by Jesus' love, you will find yourself pregnant with the power of the Holy Spirit and the desire to communicate His marvelous love to others. This is how revival begins.

It's fire we want, for fire we plead,
Send the fire!
The fire will meet our every need,
Send the fire today!
Look down and see this waiting host,
And send the promised Holy Ghost!
We need another Pentecost,
Send the fire today!

General William Booth
Founder of the Salvation Army

9 - NURTURING
THE BLESSING

As I began to yield to Him, one night I pictured Jesus standing at a doorway knocking on the door. But instead of wearing a flowing robe, He wore plumber's work clothes. Around His neck hung cables and chains. In each hand He held a toolbox. On His feet He wore muddy work boots. He was coming to fix things in people's lives in our congregation.

In this picture, I had just had neutral-colored carpet installed on the floor of a large room which I thought was part of my house. But here was Jesus with muddy boots wanting to come through the door! I wanted badly for Him to come in, but not like that! Where was the beautiful Jesus with light, glory and cleanliness? Instead, I saw that I had the impulse to put down plastic on the carpet in front of Him.

Then I realized that I was so proud that I found myself telling the Lord of glory where He could and could not step in His own house. He was coming to help me, but with "no beauty that we should desire him." (Isaiah 53:2, KJV) I realized I could make the same mistake the Pharisees did: not recognizing Jesus because He was not as I thought He should be.

No, I said, *I would much rather have the muddy footprints of Jesus than no footprints at all.*

Are you ready for Jesus to come in and repair your heart? Are you ready, pastor, for Jesus to use whatever means He wants to awaken your sleepy congregation? Opening the door to Jesus in this renewal may cost you. Some people will not understand it and will never accept it. Revival comes on God's terms, not ours. "God in revival does not take sides," said John Wesley (quoted in Robert Tuttle's John Wesley: His Life and Theology, Zondervan/Asbury, 1978). "He takes over." Isn't it time that the Lord's leaders let Him have control of His Church again?

Jumping into the River of God means letting go of control. It involves risk. But then, everything worth having—-including the visitation presence of the Lord—involves risk. All we need to know is that it is God. After that, there should be no question as to whether we surrender.

The Lord's special visitation to His Church is the most precious commodity of the Kingdom of God on earth, the pearl of great price, because it is Him. While there are different dimensions of the Lord's presence within the Church, those times when He invades our order and sets up His own are moments of power so precious that those who experience them remember them for the rest of their lives.

Recognizing a visitation and facilitating God's agenda set the heart of the true leader apart from the hireling. (see John 10:12-13) After all, it is not our Church; it is His. We are His servants, not His managers. We must be stewards of the "mysteries of God." (I Corinthians 4:1)—including the mystery of revival. What God is able to do in any local church or city, during this or any season of renewal, depends on the discerning, faithful responses of servant "leaders" who have learned above all to get out of His way and let Him move. It is for such leaders that this chapter is directed.

"Make Me Comfortable"

Rick is senior pastor of a church in Tucson, AZ. He made a habit of telling the congregation to relax and feel comfortable in worship. Concerned not to threaten the comfort zones of the large numbers of non-Christian visitors to the services, he often said from the pulpit, "Some will be dancing, some will be raising their hands, but you do whatever makes you feel comfortable."

His son, Steve, the worship leader and minister of music, saw no problem with this approach. But this was about to change.

Steve was flying home from a Vineyard worship conference in Anaheim, CA and talking with the Lord about worship in the church, when twenty minutes out of Tucson, the Lord began to respond: Your comfort is not what makes Me happy. Let me show you how it feels.

At that moment, sitting in his window seat, Steve began to laugh hysterically. Trying to conceal what was happening from the woman in the seat next to him, he hid his face in the window. That worked for ten minutes. Then the Holy Spirit overcame him so powerfully that he could not contain his laughter.

By this time he was attracting the attention of the flight attendants, one of whom offered him lozenges, apparently thinking that he had been drinking. The Lord said to him, Are you comfortable now?

By the time the passengers were were deplaning, Steve was laughing so hard he had to be helped to the door by the attendants. Then he was on his own. He made it to the end of the ramp, but collapsed to the floor at the gate where his parents were waiting.

Rick, his dad, a conservative, dignified senior pastor, told Steve later that all he wanted to do was get out of there. The waiting area was crammed with people; but the grace of God came on Rick, and he laid his hand on his son and began to pray.

At that moment a couple they did not know came up to them, while Steve was still convulsing with laughter and said, "He must have been to the Vineyard conference." Soon people in the terminal started breaking out in laughter many of them presumably unbelievers. (They were not as offended by the manifestation of laughter as many Christians would have been.)

What did this pastor and worship leader take away from this experience? Just before the plane landed, the Lord said to Steve, It's not what makes you feel comfortable; it's what makes Me feel comfortable. Then Steve realized that church leaders are to create an atmosphere in the church that is comfortable for the Lord, and that He will bring the blessing they desire.

How often have we treated the Holy Spirit like a "crazed" relative who must be kept locked in the attic? Why do we move what He does to the basement or on another night? What if we let Him out of the box we have built for Him? Perhaps more of the supernatural elements of Christianity would return to the Church?

King David's Lesson

God is speaking to leaders today in the same way He spoke to King David when he tried to bring the ark of the covenant back to Jerusalem on an oxcart. Without asking the counsel of the priests or following God's instructions in scripture for transporting this sacred piece of tabernacle furniture (see Exodus 25:13-15), David committed one of the greatest sins Christian leaders or anyone else can commit: the sin of assuming.

Placing the gold-plated ark, the symbol of God's presence on a brand new man made conveyance seemed like a convenient, even respectful way to transport the ark back to Jerusalem. No one would get tired carrying it, and everyone would then be free to participate in the celebration.

David planned the festivities and looked forward to the day the Lord's presence would return to Jerusalem. From childhood he had been a worshipper and seeker of the Lord. No doubt He took pleasure in being the leader under whose direction the glory of God would return.

The festive parade began—instruments playing, people cheering, worshipping, dancing, singing. Then, without warning, the oxen stumbled on the rough terrain. The precious ark began to slide. Acting instinctively to prevent its fall, a man named Uzzah lunged for the ark to help it back onto the cart. Instantly he fell dead.

Suddenly the festivities came to an abrupt halt. Fear and anger filled David's heart. Not only had the Lord not blessed the celebration, but His "outburst" (2 Samuel 6:8) had claimed the life of one of David's subjects. The king cried out, "How then can the ark of the Lord come to me?" (verse 9)

Until learning the answer, he decided to leave the troublesome piece of furniture, protected jealously by God's power, in the house of one of the priests. It would be three months before David had the courage to try again.

We will pickup the story again later in this chapter. But the lesson David learned was that God's ways were above his. No amount of good intentions could compensate for David's failure to find out how God wanted to return the Ark.

Sometimes the Church comes to think that God doesn't mind and that anything goes. We may think God does not really care how we do things, so long as our intentions are right. We immerse ourselves in methods that seem permissible; after all they result in good fruit, right? But when the power of God invades our lives, God challenges us with the knowledge that we cannot continue as we have. In fact, God casts our previously trusted order against the backdrop of a new awareness of what God is capable of doing so that what we are doing looks like a pitiful substitute.

Embarrassing manifestations that accompany the wonderful blessings of this current revival can produce similar effects to the Lord's horrifying "outburst" in David's procession: Some people are frightened and some are put off and angry. God is testing the Church to see if we are willing to make room for Him regardless of the cost.

Are we willing to alter our programs to allow the Holy Spirit to move as He wills? When the Church finds the precious seed of revival, we need to make the soil fertile to bear the fullest fruit. But you must count the cost.

The Cost: Giving Up Control

God is not an abusive Father, so temperamental and difficult to please that we must walk on eggshells to keep from offending

Him. Is having His Presence important enough to risk offending people and perhaps losing them?

People naturally resist change. Those who are nervous about losing control cover their real emotional condition by searching the scriptures to support their position that the changes being made are not godly. These are the people Jesus spoke about who taste the new wine and say, "The old is good enough." (Luke 5:39)

Leaders must be confident that they are acting out of obedience to the Lord, yet gentle in their approach to parishioners. This is no time to display arrogance or to imply that anyone reluctant to "jump in the River" has a "religious spirit" or does not love God. Many believers sincerely need time to process what they are seeing, examine the scriptures, be assured that it is God moving and open themselves to Him.

But there will be frustrating times when leaders must press ahead for the sake of those who long for more, while continuing to refrain from judging those who do not accept the new thing God is doing. You cannot sacrifice the hungry sheep for those who prefer to stay behind, no more than Joshua could sacrifice fully entering the promised land because Reuben, Gad and the half-tribe of Manasseh wanted to set up camp near the door.

Leaders who fear losing givers or church members will drag their feet until the visitation passes, hoping to avoid controversy. Note the following observation made by Jonathan Edwards in the eighteenth century about people who spend too long waiting to see the outcome and try to inspect every detail before committing themselves to receiving the benefits of revival:

> It is probable that many of those who are thus waiting know not for what they are waiting. If they wait to see a work of God without difficulties and stumbling blocks, it will be like a fool's waiting by the river side to have all the water run by. A work of God without stumbling blocks is never to be expected. "It must needs be that the offenses come." There never yet was any great manifestation that God made of himself to the world, without

many difficulties attending it. *Distinguishing Marks of A Work of the Spirit of God,* p.133.

Other leaders may be proud of their liturgy or order of service and enjoy retaining firm control. While resisting a new move of God, they may throw the reason off on trying not to offend people, while the real reason is that they prize their pulpits. Ask yourself, Are the services of my church merely venues for creative expression, or are they places where people may be filled with the Holy Spirit?

During a renewal meeting at his church in England, one friend of ours who was a pastor received prayer. Suddenly he found himself on the floor making swimming motions to the amusement of the members of his congregation. He was seeing a vision of himself swimming in Ezekiel's river. But as he swam, he heard the Lord say, Get your feet off the bottom. From his years as a physical education instructor, he had seen children who were keeping one foot glued to the bottom of the pool.

Likewise, for many years pastors and leaders who have looked as though they were swimming were still keeping one foot on the bottom.

The Lord continued, For many years you've stepped in and stepped onto the bottom and retained control. Now get your feet off the bottom. I want to be in control. I want this river to take you where I want you to go.

Indeed, control within a group of Christians is one of the major blockages to a move of the Holy Spirit within a congregation whether exercised by a pastor or the members. Your attempts to maintain a secure position may work for a while, but you cannot continue to be active in what God is doing without releasing yourself to the flow and trusting Him to take you where He wants you and your congregation to go.

While some pastors feel an obligation to everyone in the flock, particularly those who have supported them and contributed to the church throughout the years, our first responsibility is to honor and please God, while being patient enough with our flocks to minimize conflict. We must also face the fact that the only sheep we really have are God's, and the sheep He has allotted to our care are only the ones who trust us enough to respond to our leadership. The rest of those in the pews are merely spectators. If they neither hear nor trust you about a matter of importance like this, they will eventually leave the church anyway, and probably over something trivial.

John Arnott knows the problem well. Since the renewal began, his congregation (now called Catch the Fire) has lost members who could not accommodate the host of changes, whether in the manifestations of the renewal or in the altering of the church schedule. He observes, however, that regardless of whether the leadership opens a church to renewal, they run the risk of losing people—-either those who do not want renewal and seek out a church where they are comfortable, or those who do want renewal, do not see it happening and move on to a church open to it.

When faced with this choice, then, shouldn't a pastor choose the visitation presence of the Lord? Once you have acknowledged that a work of renewal is authored by God, how can you honestly refuse Him the right of His authority over "your" flock? That would be an abuse of authority. The decision to open your fellowship and ministry to the power of the Holy Spirit may be costly, but the cost of not doing it is even greater: missing your day of visitation and keeping others from entering in, too. No leader who genuinely loves and trusts God wants that.

Strong leadership involves wise risk-taking. The only things in life worth having are obtained by stepping out of your security zone and taking some risk. And as your hunger for God increases, He will give you the courage to take the necessary risks to invite His presence, expose your congregation to His touch and enjoy the blessings of renewal.

But there are those who have deep emotional hurts and have difficulty receiving because of them. Their emotional condition requires special patience and gentle encouragement.

Encouraging Those Who Have Difficulty

Edie had been abused by her father so many times that she never laughed nor cried. Can you imagine how she must have felt when she was confronted by how the Lord was moving in this renewal? After a few weeks, she finally called me. As I spent time talking with her, she opened up about her fears. I prayed for her, but several more months passed as she inched her way gingerly toward the River. Everyone in the congregation who knew Edie let her alone and allowed her to come when she was ready.

She received her first touch of power after the Lord had been moving in every one of our services for eight months! How happy we were to see her lying on the floor laughing under the influence of the Holy Spirit! She gave a testimony the very next night about how the Lord had gradually led her to the place where she could receive His touch. She was filled with boldness to be able to speak publicly about it. Her testimony put us in awe of the Lord's patient hand.

It is important for us to continue demonstrating love for people who are not yet able, for one reason or another, to accept what God is doing or to receive the way we do. Some of them are frightened lambs quivering from fear in the corner of the pasture. Let them understand that they are receiving more than they realize by simply sitting in the congregation, and that you appreciate their faithfulness. Do your best to break down barriers so they do not feel isolated. Some will still not respond, but you will know that you have tried your best.

As our friend from England, Gerald Coates said, "God stated His purpose in Acts was to touch Jerusalem, Judea, Samaria and the uttermost parts of the earth. If all we want is to bless our little congregation or ministry, and give us a super-duper version of what we had before we will be disappointed. God is changing things up, challenging our strengths, strengthening our weaknesses, making us more dependent on Him, because there is something new that He wants to do. Like Isaiah 43:19, 'I am doing a new thing...will you not perceive it?'...the answer is "no, we don't."

Do you realize why your congregation exists? And what does this moving of the Spirit have to do with the "vision" God has given you? Maybe what you think is a vision is really ambition. If it is, He may throw it in the trash, or He may prune it radically so that it can bear fruit.

Another question you may face is whether or not your congregation should attempt protracted meetings. Perhaps your congregation may be a refreshing center for the local area or it may be a place that reaches out to touch the lost.

In 1994, the Toronto church saw its crowds increase by 1,500 to 2,000 outside visitors a night since the outpouring began. Conferences escalated the attendance to more than 5,000 outside visitors. The cost this church has paid to freely bless the worldwide body of Christ staggers anyone who is familiar with church administration. But the visitation has blessed this church in return.

Facing Why I Really Want Revival

The churches who will become refreshing centers, however, are few. I must confess that, although I really wanted revival for the right reasons, unfortunately there were times when I wanted it for the wrong ones. After we had suffered in smallness and borne the brunt of people rejecting us because we weren't larger and had all the programs in place, I longed for revival because I envisioned that it would improve our natural situation. I hoped our church would grow larger and that we would see an influx of new believers to add momentum in order to break the cycle of sameness. New givers would be great, too, or so I thought. But alas it was not to be.

After we had embraced and held the renewal out on an open hand for over ten years, and after we had had over 30,000 people walk through our doors to attend the Friday night renewal meetings for at least eight of those years, our church did not grow substantially. However, the work of the Holy Spirit among us became one of maturity. The Lord pruned the congregation in 2004. The means He used to accomplish this pruning was a church split. I will spare you the unfortunate details, but the wounds from it were some of the most hurtful of my life. At this writing, all who originally left are at peace with us and Bill and I are healed. It not longer hurts, but we did learn powerful lessons which God could not have taught us any other way.

The people who remained with us have since grown spiritually to the degree that they genuinely love each other and are similar to a community which is now a family. I truly love them. They are not the "50 pounds of souls" which I ordered from God at the "altar deli." In response to my prayers and longings, I believe God gave us people with whom we have been able to walk through the storms of life and come out still loving Jesus more than anything else.

There are times we fellowship with each other and reminisce about the early days of renewal, and there are still the occasional manifestations and an outbreak of holy laughter here and there, but the people here now are more a model of the first century church than any I have ever seen. Now we are beginning to feel the revival breeze in the tops of the trees, but it is no longer our primary focus. Jesus is. I believe that this is true Christianity.

Whatever the Lord calls your church congregation to do, He will reveal His purpose for it one day at a time. Meanwhile, there is no limit to the amount of joy He will dispense to any Christian hungry for more. But our contentment must be found in intimacy with God, and He may test your motives as you allow Him to reveal why you want revival. Is it to build His Kingdom or your own? Are you possessed with a sectarian/denominational spirit? Or is to create a ministry with your brand on it? Jesus soundly condemned these motives when He rebuked the Pharisees for "wanting the chief seats at banquets, respectful greetings in the marketplaces and being called 'rabbi.'" These are not Kingdom values. They are the opposite of humility and gentleness and especially devoid of love which esteems the other brother as more important than yourself. It amounts to "using" people and "using" the move of God for your own end.

Ask God to purify your motives and give you a desire for the simplicity and purity of knowing Jesus Christ. Whatever you do, do not disguise your lust for more as coming from God.

Regardless of His purpose for your congregation or your ministry, it is important that you open yourself to the continuous blessing of the Spirit. Honor the way God has chosen to come by opening your door to this phase of the moving of the Holy Spirit. It will prove foundational for whatever God does next in revival, but it will only do so if you remain in a constant state of spiritual hunger and eager response to what God is doing.

The Leader As A Receiver And Participant

Back to King David now...He was not only a dynamic leader but humble before God. When the order of the Lord was finally secured and he felt ready to transport the Ark to Jerusalem, he set aside his kingly robes, put on the simple white garment of a priest and began to worship the Lord along with everyone else, "dancing before the Lord with all his might" and dancing before the nation as well. (2 Samuel 6:14)

The Lord loves nothing better than to see his ministers leading their flocks into the wonderful refreshing of renewal by receiving the blessing themselves—in front of their people.

Pastor Rick, of the thriving church in Tucson, AZ whose son was taken with laughter while getting off the plane, had been teaching a four-hour class in another part of the church. Afterward, he opened a door to enter the sanctuary during a service where the Holy Spirit was being poured out on the youth of the church. There in front of him was a somber young man who previously had given little outward sign of involvement. Now he was drunk in the Spirit and was standing in Pastor Rick's path. When he touched the young man on the shoulder, Pastor Rick, normally a very conservative personality, found himself at the front of the auditorium, sliding down the wall of the sanctuary, collapsing to the floor, laughing hysterically. Every time he thought it was over, he tried to stand up and another wave hit him. It felt to Rick as if he had been slain in the Spirit. A wave of peace swept over him and the joy of the Lord welled up inside. This went on for a half-hour as the youthful congregation looked on, enjoying every moment of it.

"It was the Lord making a statement to the church," he says, "that what He wanted to do was OK. They know me and they trust me."

A leader runs the risk of being misunderstood, losing the respect of the more dignified in the congregation. King David danced so hard in front of the Lord as he was anointed by the Holy Spirit that he embarrassed his wife Michal. The daughter of David's predecessor, Saul, Michal believed she knew, from being reared in Saul's family, the proper demeanor of royalty. Now in anger she shamed David, mocking him sarcastically: "How the king of Israel distinguished himself today! He uncovered himself today in the eyes of his servants' maids as one of the foolish ones shamelessly uncovers himself!" (2 Samuel 6:20)

David replied,

It was before the Lord, who chose me above your father and above all his house, to appoint me ruler over the people of the Lord, over Israel; therefore I will celebrate before the Lord. And I will be more lightly esteemed than this and will be humble in my own eyes, but with the maids of whom you have spoken, I will be distinguished. (Verses 21-22)

The text follows with this fearful observation, "Michal the daughter of Saul had no child to the day of her death." (Verse 23)

Is it possible that our own spiritual barrenness has been partly the result of our unwillingness to let the Holy Spirit have control of us in front of others?

When theologian, Dr. R. T. Kendall, who was pastor, now retired, of London's Westminster Chapel and the one who "carried" the blessing to Stuart Bell, received prayer, the Holy Spirit came, causing him to fall in front of his deacons. He wondered why

God chose to move on him in front of them. Could not God have allowed him to receive in private? But he concluded as he told Alive Church in Lincoln, that God wanted to humble him.

What distinguishes a leader in God's sight is preferring His presence and approval above the opinions of those he or she leads. Do not allow anyone to quench the Spirit in you, or condemn you for opening your heart to the Holy Spirit or for receiving the blessings of renewal. Some will mock your hunger and say that you are "too needy." Others will accuse you of being "sucked into deception." The tragedy is that people who say things like this are cursing themselves with a form of spiritual barrenness because they have yet to appreciate their own need for the Holy Spirit's presence and power.

But let's make certain we always maintain our need for Him— or else, face the next move of God with a hardened heart, blinded by pride and find ourselves in the critics' camp, never realizing we are rejecting the blessing of the Lord because, like Michal, we cannot forget the good old days. Only as we continue to receive will we be able to discern and pastor in the renewal adequately.

Allowing Powerful Honest Testimony

The sense of awe that accompanies true revival has the capacity to draw others to Jesus. It was present in the first century after the Holy Spirit fell in Jerusalem. Luke described the atmosphere in the book of Acts:

> They were continually devoting themselves to the apostles' teaching and to fellowship, to the breaking of bread and to prayer. And everyone kept feeling a sense of awe, and many wonders and signs were taking place through the apostles. (Acts 2:42-43)

Business as usual is normally devoid of awe, and it is possible to take the Lord's wonders for granted. When it becomes commonplace to see laughing in the Spirit and people falling under the power of the Spirit, the sense of the awe will diminish before long. So we must guard the refreshing sense of the Lord's presence that causes believers to long after Him so single-mindedly that they sacrifice ordinary pursuits to be in His presence.

When I asked pastors in Britain and the US about sustaining a move of the Holy Spirit, almost all of them spoke of the power of an honest testimony from members of the congregation or even from newcomers being touched as the key to nurturing the blessing. "Let the redeemed of the Lord say so, whom He has redeemed from the hand of the enemy." (Psalm 107:2, NKJV) When believers who are experiencing a lull in spiritual activity hear of God touching others who are receiving, they are encouraged to learn that God has not withdrawn the sense of His Presence simply because they are having a bad day.

But the testimonies must be honest and genuine. Nothing deflates a person more than to learn that what he thought was a supernatural touch from God turns out to have been only temporary enthusiasm without lasting effect. Such was the case several years after the renewal began when attendees at a Toronto conference began to think that they were receiving gold fillings in their teeth supernaturally.

Scores of people were looking in each other's mouths and determining that they had received a supernatural gold filling. One of the leaders called me in Pittsburgh to invite me to the conference as I was the editor of *Spread the Fire*, Toronto's magazine. They thought I should see it to report on it. Like Kathryn Kuhlman used to do, I asked everyone to fill out a form who believed they had had a miracle. But sadly, as the attendees returned home to check with their dentists, they were disillusioned to discover that, indeed, their dental work was natural and not a miraculous work of God.

Such has been the same with "gold dust" floating through the atmosphere and appearing on people's bodies and "jewels" appearing on the floor. Was it telling that somehow the attention on Jesus that had been so palpable in the early days of the outpouring causing people to lie on the floor looking upward as though looking into His face were now looking downward onto man and to the floor? I am sorry to say this, but I have not seen any incontrovertible affirmation that any of this was supernatural. In fact, test after test revealed faux jewels and glitter. One woman who somehow gained access to the pulpit there was thought to be having gold dust fall from her hair during her messages. John Arnott found that the "gold dust" was glitter and canceled her remaining meetings immediately.

The awe of God is a fragile thing, a treasure. We must guard it ruthlessly. The Holy Spirit never uses trust in what is false to "lead people into all truth." God is not offended when we look for what is true. Trying to believe the false quenches the Holy Spirit, in favor of creating a sensation which can perpetuate a "false awe" in a meeting. But longing for Jesus and the heavenly Father's love encourages Him to do more of the real. The same is true of healings. God performs spectacular miracles of healing. However, he does not heal everyone. To pretend that one is healed when one is not healed does great harm to the Gospel of Jesus Christ.

Before the renewal began, Bill and I had become cynical and skeptical of so much of what was put forth as miraculous because it was always linked somehow to money or publicity and proved not to be lasting or false. I know what sort of harm can come to a person who is disillusioned like this. It is ok to expect confirmation and to long for the real.

"My name is Bill W..."

So when the Holy Spirit touched Bill Westerberg, we waited. Bill had been a member of our congregation previously and is the son of Nancy Westerberg, the long time children's pastor at our congregation (now retired.) Bill had once been on our worship team, but a several year long relapse into alcoholism had drained him of his desire to follow Jesus. He had not been to church more than five times in eight years. One of these times was recent, when he had come to hear his mother testify that she had been touched by the Lord's renewing presence. Almost reluctantly Bill came forward for prayer. Nothing outward happened. Two weeks went by.

On Saturday morning, the phone rang, it was Bill. He told me that in the two weeks since receiving prayer, his mind had been filled with promises the Lord had made to him while he had been walking with Him more closely. He could not get these promises out of his thoughts.

"Do you think now could be the time God will start moving in my life?" he asked me.

I do not recommend my response to him as a counseling model; I can only tell you what I did. I started to laugh, and I kept laughing as long as Bill kept talking. Nevertheless, by the end of the conversation (which admittedly had become one-sided), Bill seemed somewhat lifted. Bill was always a depressive alcoholic, and when he was drinking he became somber, moody, pessimistic and depressed.

That same evening, Bill phoned back with the following account of his day:

After his conversation with me that morning, he "reasoned" that if that were his last day to drink, he would make a day of it. So he did, drinking all that Saturday in the upstairs apartment he was renting in his sister's house.

About seven o'clock that evening he began to laugh. In fact, he could not stop laughing. He laughed so hard that he was afraid his sister, Debra, downstairs would hear him, so he stuck his head under the couch to muffle the sound. She came trotting upstairs anyway.

"Bill," she exclaimed, "what's wrong with you?" Looking at the empty bottle on his kitchen table, she said, "I am calling an ambulance to take you to detox! You're drunk!"

But Bill replied, "Don't call the ambulance; there's nothing wrong with me! God is touching me and for the first time in years, I feel the love of God all over me!"

And so the love of God was drawing Bill back to Himself.

He sobered up instantly. The holy laughter that was making everyone else drunk made him sober! Then having regained his composure, he called my husband.The very next morning in church he gave a powerful testimony in front of the congregation—just the facts of what happened to him the day before. We know that many addicts relapse in recovery. We asked him not to extrapolate this experience into a total healing; so he didn't. He wanted to stop smoking immediately, but my husband discouraged that knowing how stopping both suddenly could sabotage his recovery. He said he wanted to come back to church. And the congregation welcomed him back with open arms.

For a few weeks, Bill was able to resist the bottle; however, one day he relapsed. In fact, he relapsed off and on for awhile. But this time, instead of running from God's love, he kept coming back for prayer. He decided that this time he was not letting go of the Lord. He started attending AA. Now his "Higher Power" was the real Higher Power, the Holy Spirit. The Lord enabled him to lay down both tobacco and alcohol and never pick them up again. He was able to let go because he was continually filled with God's new wine!

That was 26 years ago (from time of this writing in 2021). Today Bill's testimony is *"I will always remember that day when God touched me. I continue to ask God for a new revelation of His love and to enable me to receive it. The times of refreshing will always be a special time in my life. I am now confident that 'He who began a good work in me will bring it to completion.'"*

Bill's testimony is, for me, one of the most powerful of the renewal because it is honest. He did not need to exaggerate because it was real. His healing and deliverance from alcohol has been an encouragement to others to trust in a God who can do what men could not. His was one of the testimonies that fulfilled God's promise to us that day when the tongue and interpretation rang out, "I want to come in the church and do things you have never seen me do before, touch people in ways you have never seen Me touch them before and use people you have never seen me use before; and all I want to know is 'do I have your permission?'"

Testimonies don't need 'spin.' For Bill to have testified the first day that he had been "totally delivered from alcohol" would have brought reproach to the Gospel when he experienced relapse. But now Bill's testimony is more powerful, because it has proven true by standing the test of time. God's miracles last and although apparently everyone whom Jesus healed eventually died, they were truly healed and the signs and wonders He performed drew thousands by word of mouth.

Allowing people to testify can be risky as in the case of one woman who came to a meeting in Toronto. She was in awe of how God touched her. She was not schooled in proper testifying and described her entrance into the meeting this way, "I didn't know what the hell was going on here when I walked in, but ..." Awe can be transmitted even through raw observations!

Try to have people testify simply without irrelevant details and share how the experience pointed them to Jesus and the Father's love. As they finish, pray for them and allow them to receive more from the Lord. If we are so perfectionistic that we cannot allow for people's foibles, we can quench the Holy Spirit and people will be afraid of testifying.

Is It Right To Correct Someone If...?

Nurturing the blessing does not mean that we throw out either our brains or our Bibles. Bringing the word of God and the scripture into the moving of the Holy Spirit brings balance. There must be both attention to the word of God and to the Holy Spirit because they are in agreement. It is also important to give people a biblical handle for the manifestations that are occurring. Don't be afraid to search them out. There is scriptural basis for them all—and a few extra ones that have not happened, so far! Teaching from scripture also places a move of God in perspective and answers questions about its place in God's plan as we learn what that is.

However, anything that stanches the way the Holy Spirit wants to bless His Church needs to be avoided.

Early in the renewal, John Arnott made a decision not to

prune too quickly. A few years before, revival had broken out among the youth of his congregation. Afraid that things were getting "flaky" and out of hand, he tried to bring correction. The revival was short-lived. Later as he sought the Lord, God showed him that he had quenched the Holy Spirit through his overeagerness to correct. He promised the Lord then that if he was granted another opportunity, he would give much more latitude to the Spirit.

Leaders must make up their minds early that their own comfort zones are less important than enabling the flock to shed its fears and receive from God. Some people are so inhibited that as soon as they let themselves go and surrender to the Lord, they have pangs of regret, afraid they have allowed themselves too much freedom. These are not the ones who need correction! If anything, they need a wide space and much encouragement to be free in the Spirit. Watching the leaders respond to the Spirit will encourage them.

During the renewal meetings in our congregation, every so often a person we didn't know would launch out with a word of prophecy. We gently asked them to hold the word, not because it wasn't real, but because we simply didn't know them. Why is that important? The scripture indicates that we are to "know those who labor among you." We have no way of knowing their character or intent. It is important to know the vessels from whom gifts are flowing because "many false prophets are out there in the world." When the porch light cuts on, it draws the guests but also the bugs! The Holy Spirit is not offended and is able to hold it if necessary and honors the congregation and its servant leaders.

Pruning The Flesh Or Quenching The Holy Spirit?

But how will I know if I am pruning the excess or quenching the Holy Spirit? It is probably better to do nothing until you are relatively certain which it is. One way to tell is by asking the person to describe what is going on with them. If the Holy Spirit is at work, there will be positive fruit: an inner healing, a physical healing, a greater love for the Father or passion for Jesus. When the fruit of the Spirit is not present, that is the time to correct, especially when true experiences of the Spirit are mocked or imitated in a way that belittles them.

I was the guest speaker at a women's retreat in Maryland in May of 1995. The Holy Spirit poured out in an amazing way through the ministry team. It was the first time many of the attendees had been exposed to this new wave of the Holy Spirit. About 90% of the women were touched to the degree that they were 'slain in the Spirit.' All the outward manifestations appeared: some were shaking, some women were frozen in place. During the ministry time, one of the prayer team members was able to lead a woman to Jesus. She was actually the mother of a Methodist minister whose family had been praying for her for a long time. The Holy Spirit was clearly moving when a woman towards the back of the room started causing a commotion. There was a frown on her face and she resembled someone in a trance. She kept saying, "Don't touch me; don't touch me," as the ministry team tried to pray for her. Her anger and rebellion was causing her to scowl and resist co-operating with the otherwise happy pandemonium everyone else was experiencing. She kept up her resistance as I approached her, too. Finally, she finally had to be removed from the room.

In another meeting we were having with two other churches in Pittsburgh, it was prayer time and one fellow started running so fast around the room that he nearly stumbled over those on the floor. My husband cautioned him to slow down. He didn't comply thinking that he was "moving in the Spirit." Not five minutes later, he ran into a wall and broke his wrist. Was it the judgment of God? No, he was just suffering the effects of poor judgment.

No doubt, there are those who develop habits of responding whenever they sense the Holy Spirit's presence. One man in our congregation came to believe that he was making a sound that resembled the sound of an eagle. (It was more like the caw of a crow.) One night, my husband recorded 50 times that he made the noise during one message. Bill made a breakfast appointment and talked to him about it. My husband is a gentle man and far from being arrogant and rough. However, this fellow maintained that it was all the Holy Spirit and wound up leaving the congregation because he was offended and thought my husband was "quenching the Holy Spirit." It was sad because we genuinely loved this family. I heard John Arnott ask his congregation to give him the latitude of making a mistake in case he quenched something that was truly the Holy Spirit. Remember that the Holy Spirit knows everything-even what it is genuine and what is not.

Some "habits" are less intrusive, but after a time, they will stop. They are no cause for alarm or correction unless they are accompanied by a "look at me" attitude. The Holy Spirit is the epitome of humility. His goal is not to draw attention to Himself, but to the Father and the Son. The long term effects of the Holy Spirit are often not visible unless one is looking for them. And then they are full of love, joy, peace and all the other fruit mentioned in Scripture.

As time goes by, newcomers may come and react to the touch of God in the same way you did at the beginning. Allow it. Find a place for them to enjoy God without disrupting the rest of what the Holy Spirit is doing. Have the ministry team lay hands on people and pray for them, asking the Lord to help them understand what it is that He wants them to receive.

But What About Unbelievers?

Let them come, and welcome them. They are likely not to be as offended as churchgoers.

Stuart Bell describes a meeting at his downtown church building in Lincoln, England where the Holy Spirit moved powerfully. A number of people received prayer. As they left the building they were falling under the influence of the Spirit to the point that they were lying on the sidewalk and crawling on the steps. You can imagine the effect this had on passersby. Not long afterward, the owner of a local pub came to the church and said, "I had to see what was going on. There's more happening here than in my pub!"

Signs and wonders and manifestations confront unbelievers with the power of the real God. Evidently God thinks so, or He would not have poured out the Holy Spirit the way He did on Pentecost. We need to stop being embarrassed for God. Let Him be in control of what people see and do not see. Have someone sit with them if they want and explain what is happening. Sometimes they will not come back, but as long as what is going on in the services is genuine, isn't that between them and God?

There is no more powerful effect on an unbeliever than seeing a once-dead church revived. It is the most powerful testimony of all. Let them hear testimonies of how God is moving in people's lives. This plants a seed that will remain in their hearts (as it did with Bill Westerberg's) until they open them completely to the Lord.

Another by-product of the outpouring came in the Anglican Church in Britain. One of its most fruitful tools of evangelism is the Alpha course, a ten-week course for inquirers into the Christian faith that started several years prior to the renewal at Holy Trinity, Brompton. By 1995 the effects of the Toronto outpouring were visible having seen over 1,600 Alpha courses spring up all over the body of Christ. At HTB every Wednesday night, more than 500 people gathered for Alpha. People from every walk of life from a homeless person who formerly lay on the sidewalk outside the church to a banker in the financial district have come to Jesus Christ and have become active in the congregation through Alpha. The fish are biting out there.

The House Of Obed-Edom

After David first attempted to restore the Ark of the Covenant to Jerusalem and failed, he set it aside in the house of Obed-Edom, the Gittite. After three months, David apparently sent word to find out how things were going. Perhaps after the death of Uzza, who had tried to steady the ark, David expected to find a pile of body bags outside Obed-Edom's house! But to his delight, the courier told him the news that "the Lord had blessed the house of Obed-Edom and all that belongs to him, on account of the Ark of God." (2 Samuel 6:12)

God's blessing on Obed-Edom's house encouraged David to take the Ark home with him. He built what is known as the Tabernacle of David, a simple tent pitched around the Ark practically in his own backyard. He wanted the same blessing. This time he made sure that the priests carried it on their shoulders.

What had happened to Obed-Edom while the Ark of the Covenant was in his house? In that short time period, he became attached to the presence of the Lord. In addition, the Lord began to multiply his house. David appointed Obed-Edom as one who worshipped the Lord day and night before the Ark. As Obed-Edom worshipped, he was given new realms of responsibility. His household was put in charge as gatekeepers of the storehouse, then as caretakers of the treasury and of the vessels of ministry. David saw that since Obed-Edom could be trusted with the Ark, he could be trusted with anything. He became a man whose household lived in the presence of God.

God does not simply want to "visit," He longs for people and congregations in which He can dwell. These places value Him more than their own agendas. Like the house of Obed-Edom, they remain faithful to Him, to the simplicity and purity of knowing Jesus because they love Jesus Christ. These are they who nurture the blessing.

But how can I guard what God has entrusted to me personally, especially if I am in a congregation that doesn't?

10 - GUARDING YOUR OIL

The renewal had been flourishing in our congregation for ten months with only mild ebbs and flows, until one week in the fall of 1995. It seemed like that week a heavy weight dropped onto the church.

We have never believed in placing undue emphasis on the enemy, nor do we look for him behind every mishap. But suddenly he over played his hand and launched a discernible attack. That Sunday more than half the congregation, for one reason or another, failed to show up for Sunday service. One family was suffering because the father had lost his job. Many others were suffering a lull, too. Several were succumbing to depression.

For months I had enjoyed unbroken communion with the Lord. An air of expectancy had pervaded my spirit. This week, however, when I started to pray, I felt like I was praying through molasses. I kept sighing from a weight that seemed to have fallen on me.

Bill felt it, too. It was as though we were suddenly carrying the full burden alone again. The devil, it seemed, was snickering in the corner, sticking out his tongue at us as though daring us to rise above the messes he had secretly created.

Four months earlier, the congregation had received a prophetic word: "Keep the fire lit, for it is about to catch on in your area." After ten months of continuous blessing, we had heard of only five other local congregations (three of them, small, like ours) that had been affected by the renewal. In several other churches in the area, renewal had begun but had fizzled or been stamped out by opposition. Our congregation seemed like a small pilot light on a gas range. Needed was an open valve in a few more churches and a surge of the Lord's presence for the fire to catch on in the Pittsburgh area. But it was difficult to remain enthusiastic and hold on for the next phase of God's blessing.

Throughout the year, Bill and I had made eight trips to Toronto, just for the purpose of fanning the flame of love for Jesus in our own hearts. Every time we went, the Lord met us with tender encouragement. Now it was time to guard what He had entrusted to us. But how?

Identifying The Opposition

The parable of the ten virgins waiting for the bridegroom in Matthew 25 carries a clear message to any church or individual believer who has been blessed with the fresh oil of renewal. "When the foolish took their lamps," said Jesus, "they took no oil with them, but the prudent took oil in flasks along with their lamps." (Verses 3-4)

This parable, which describes the door of the wedding feast being shut to the five foolish virgins who ran out of oil, seems strong coming from the lips of Jesus, but it is a prophetic warning to anyone who has received the oil of joy for his lamp: Guard that oil! The weapons formed against this renewal are the same that attack every move of the Holy Spirit. Satan is not very original. He does not have to be; we are too often ignorant of his schemes. Here are three main weapons he uses:

Public Denunciation

Anyone who has experienced a revived passion for Jesus, His work and His people will face ridicule, criticism and public opposition from brothers and sisters. Similarly, in the days following Israel's return from captivity, Sanballat, Tobiah and Gesham purported to favor what was right but opposed Nehemiah's project to rebuild the wall around Jerusalem.

I am not talking about the honest seeker who does not yet

understand what God is doing, but the self-satisfied religionist who, without hungering earnestly for more and searching until he finds, sets himself in vociferous opposition. He may even make a livelihood from engendering controversy in the Body of Christ through a "ministry" of what amounts to little more than fault-finding and backbiting. This person may be a "Herod" who tells the wise men searching for the baby Jesus to "go and find him for me," (Matthew 2:8) and who makes a pretense of wanting to worship when he really wants to destroy.

Such opposition can be a sign that the situation being debated is a genuine work of God. In general, the more powerful the truth, the stronger the criticism. But those who enjoy controversy may find the effects of renewal ebbing from their own spirits.

Opposition can also ensnare those who feel they must protect a work of God from slander. Soon they are drawn into wrestling with flesh and blood—what Paul said we are not struggling against (see Ephesians 6:12). It is best to let the opponents alone, avoid dissension and seek only Jesus.

When Stephen prayed for those who were stoning him to death, his intercessory pleas for forgiveness included mercy for "a young man named Saul" (Acts 7:58) who held the cloaks of Stephen's murderers. Did Stephen's prayer for forgiveness contribute to Saul's salvation? Perhaps. And you are probably a Christian today partially because of the influence of Saul, who later penned a large portion of the New Testament.

Facing opposition within a local congregation is the more difficult, in my opinion, and needs to be confronted by the leadership within a local congregation. In a large church it is more difficult for opposing voices to gain influence, but in a smaller one they are heard more easily. The pastors and leaders may need to speak with those who are hostile or bitter.

Charles Finney, America's foremost revival preacher in the nineteenth century, warned about being drawn into controversy with opponents:

Revivals can be put down by the combined opposition of the Old School, and a bad spirit in the New School. If those who do nothing to promote revivals continue their opposition, and if those who are laboring to promote them allow themselves to get impatient, and get into a bad spirit, the revival will cease. When the Old School write letters in the newspapers, against revivals or revival men, and the New School write letters back again, in an angry, contentious spirit, revivals will cease....Let them keep about their work, and neither talk about the opposition, nor preach upon it, nor rush into print about it. If others choose to publish "slang," let the Lord's people keep to their work. None of the slander will stop the revival while those who are engaged in it mind their business, and keep to the work... *Finney on Revival* (Bethany, 1994), pp. 63-64

Remember, no one can take away your ability to be touched by your Heavenly Father unless you allow opponents or objectors to offend you. Pray for them.

Apathy

A far more subtle weapon of the enemy than public opposition is wielded within a group of people who agree that a particular blessing is from God but take the move of the Holy Spirit for granted. They believe the Lord will always be there and that their participation in renewal services is not necessary. They come and go, press the grace of God to the limit and ignore the season of blessing. They may give lip service to it, but their actions speak more loudly than their words, as if what God is doing is not real or is merely a fad that will pass.

Apathy is a more insidious and effective weapon than public denunciation. It is the sin of the Laodicean church in the book of Revelation who did not know how "wretched" they were, or that Jesus was knocking gently on the door of their hearts (see Revelation 3:14-22).

The reactions of many in the Body of Christ who do not recognize what God is doing today are similar to those of the patients in the movie, Awakenings, with Robin Williams and Robert DeNiro. It is the true story of a young psychiatrist, Dr. Oliver Sacks, who discovered in 1969 that the medication L-Dopa, normally used to treat Parkinson's disease, would awaken victims of encephalitis lethargica, known as "sleeping sickness,"out of their decades-long catatonic states. Eagerly he battled for and received permission to give the medication to his patients. And to his joy, the victims began to awaken to live normal lives. But as time wore on, the doctor watched in horror and despair as one by one they lapsed back into their silent, frozen, trancelike states. The medication proved too toxic at heavy doses and reversed its healing effects. The patients who were still "awake" were appalled at the prospect of losing the miraculous effects of the medication and reverting to their former condition.

Likewise, those who take renewal for granted or who do not treasure it enough to commit themselves wholeheartedly to the Lord's purposes will find apathy creeping into their lives and putting them back to spiritual slumber.

Revival is a precious time in the Church that happens for only rare periods. Real visitations are humanly unpredictable and may occur only once in several decades. So it is important to recognize a genuine revival, embrace it and regard it as the most precious blessings the Holy Spirit will bring to the Church in your lifetime.

If ever there was a time to serve God, it is now. It is time to deny yourself and rearrange your schedule to prioritize the work of God.

Isaiah 55 speaks to any church or believer who needs revival: "Seek the Lord while He may be found; call upon Him while He is near." (Isaiah 55:6) This implies that the Lord is nearer during certain seasons than others. The apostle Peter cautioned us to "repent therefore and return, that your sins may be wiped away, in order that times of refreshing may come from the presence of the Lord." (Acts 3:19) The phrase times of refreshing implies the same thing in the context of the New Covenant as the admonition from Isaiah does in the Old.

Even though each of us who has accepted Jesus Christ as Saviour has a deposit of the Holy Spirit within, we can also be blessed during seasons when the Lord's visitation presence draws especially near. Signs and wonders increase and the Holy Spirit moves powerfully to change lives and situations that only weeks before seemed impossible. Believers are filled with new life and joy. To ignore such a season or to partake of it with less than full devotion causes deep grief to God and discouragement to His people.

A season of visitation is not a time to "forsake our own assembling together" (Hebrews 10:25) or to substitute the mundane pursuits of life for the precious presence of the Lord. Those so tempted must remember the words of Jesus to Jerusalem: "How often I wanted to gather your children together, the way a hen gathers her chicks under her wings, and you were unwilling!" (Matthew 23:37)

The ones who make themselves continuous "receivers," who do not make trips to the altar an empty ritual, will find themselves filled and filled again with the Holy Spirit and will avoid the apathy that settles in on those who do not. And unless we make our renewal top priority, we will have trouble with the next tool of the enemy.

Discouragement

Unless we guard the presence of the Holy Spirit within, we may relapse (like the patients in Awakenings), into not only apathy but discouragement. I fear this weapon of the enemy most of all.

Before the present renewal, continual disappointment had all but quenched the Holy Spirit in me. The ministry had become a religious hell. Then the Lord sent refreshing into my heart and revived what Isaiah called "a dimly burning wick." (Isaiah 42:3)

Jack Groblewski, a pastor from Bethlehem, PA I mentioned earlier, shared in his characteristically humorous way. "Before the renewal, one day I had an elders' meeting and a dental appointment. I knew things were bad when I realized I was looking forward more to my dental appointment than the elders' meeting!"

He is not alone. Thousands of desperate pastors from all over the world have made their way to Toronto in the hopes that God would meet them. During trials of their faith, they had lost their passion for Jesus, and now they have found Him.

It is that passion for the Lord Jesus Christ, the ability to have a sustained, intimate communion with Him, that I value most about this present renewal.

When the enemy attacked that week in our congregation, ten months after the renewal started, I realized it had been nearly a year since I had been discouraged. One by one, reports of discouraging news reached our ears. The enemy seemed to be pulling out the stops against us. As each report came to our attention, I felt angry and robbed and powerless to help each person in trouble. I had no answer for them other than God's River of blessing: I knew His power could heal and cleanse them; but I could not make them keep drinking.

In the face of bad news, we fear God will abandon us to figure it all out on our own. Then Satan comes to create worst-case scenarios for our fertile minds in the form of assumptions: It will never ... I can't ... They won't ... Anger follows quickly, which we often internalize, causing depression. Finally, we spread the despair to others through vocalizing our negative assumptions.

It was difficult for me to advocate renewal when it seemed to be fading in our own congregation. It discouraged me to realize that apathy was settling in on the congregation, and that we were headed, whether we realized it or not, back to business as usual, or to a form of renewal with no substance. For several hours one day, the weight of depression remained on me. I felt like sleeping rather than working.

But I did something I never did before. I decided not to allow myself to become discouraged.

Deep in my heart, beneath all the troublesome feelings, the fire Jesus had mercifully stirred and fed for several months was still there. Through the generosity of friends, I was able to retreat to the mountains nearby and work on this book. I refused to allow discouragement to swallow my spirit and quench the flame. And as I focused my attention on all that the Lord had done in our church, and in the Body of Christ throughout the world, the problems in our congregation faded into their proper perspective.

It was then that the Lord began to speak to me and show me my heart. He had brought me out of a sense of despair which had come from trusting in the arm of flesh. Neither Bill nor I could fan the flames of renewal in our own strength. We had come to a place of abject poverty of spirit. There were no substitutes for real visitation, nor could we support it with our own efforts. It had to be a work of the Holy Spirit: "Not by might nor by power, but by My Spirit, says the Lord of hosts ..." (Zechariah 4:6) Instead of feeling despair, I felt hope, as though the Lord was giving me faith that could be tested. My discouragement, I realized, had been allowed by the Lord, who subtracted from us every other recourse but Him.

Now I knew what King David must have felt like when he returned from the battle to find the city of Ziklag pillaged and his two wives (along with the wives and children of his men) carried away into captivity. (see I Samuel 30) His men were furious at him and bitter; then David withdrew and "strengthened himself in the Lord his God." (Verse 6) Before renewal I had been unable to do this. I was more sensitive to the climate of discouragement without than the power of the Holy Spirit within. But now, in my own poverty of spirit, I had been blessed with the power of the Kingdom of heaven.

How To Guard Your Oil

What can you do when your personal supply of oil is threatened? How can you handle confrontation by the opposition of public denunciation, apathy or discouragement?

Keep Receiving

I have undergone profound emotional healing by receiving prayer during the current renewal hundreds of times. The joy

I have obtained from soaking in the River has motivated me to continue receiving prayer, which has gradually washed away fears and filled me with the Holy Spirit to a sense of fullness I have never experienced before.

I am convinced that we do not see more breakthroughs in the Church because we allow the enemy to discourage us from continued "soaking" prayer. On at least one occasion, Jesus found it necessary to lay hands on the same blind man twice before his sight was restored properly. (see Mark 8:22-26) If Jesus Himself needed to do this, why do we think we should be able to solve every problem in one "zap" of prayer?

Once again, Jesus said to keep on asking, keep on seeking, keep on knocking (see Matthew 7:7). We give up too soon.

Nurture Childlike Dependency

We discussed in the last chapter that childlikeness embraces all the positive characteristics of children and causes us to acknowledge our dependence not on human strength or cleverness but on the power of the Holy Spirit.

The same is true with dealing with opposition, apathy or discouragement. When you see yourself as a child belonging to the God who longs to hold and protect you, you submit readily to Him.

We cannot say enough about humility and childlikeness because they resist the worst sin of the human spirit, pride. Pride in the heart is subtle and can overtake you quickly, making you boast (aloud or to yourself) about what God is doing with you. Sometimes others will accuse you of pride when it is not really there; but sometimes it is there. Pride causes you to take credit for some aspect of spiritual renewal, as though your prayers brought it about or as though your sincerity were greater than that of others. Pride leads to an intensity born of effort and is the enemy of revival. Remaining childlike will guard against this.

Unfortunately, some otherwise sincere people in Toronto began to think that it was because they knew about the Father heart of God that God chose them to lead it. Attempting to assign reasons why God does what He does is arrogant. The outpouring in Pensacola, FL seemed not to have this emphasis, but God poured Himself out there almost a year and a half after He came to Toronto. Should people surmise, as did a presbyter in their denomination, that Toronto wasn't handling it well, so He poured Himself out there to 'rectify His mistake.' I remember him saying to me, "What's going on in Toronto isn't God; it's all the flesh; "this (referring to Pensacola) is God." He uttered these words sporting a black eye he had received the night before during prayer and ministry time in Pensacola when someone fell on top of him. I doubt that he was a spokesman for God or Pensacola, for that matter. However, I like John Arnott's childlike original conclusion, "Revival came here because we were near the airport."

To be childish, on the other hand, is to be proud and selfish. Instead, give away the blessing liberally with no thought for yourself or your own church.

Pride leads to a denominational or sectarian spirit, which causes you to try to capture the revival and use it for church growth or other tainted motives. Every pastor wants to see his congregation grow, but the Lord will bless the church that doesn't use its blessing to lure others. Better to bless the sheep of others and send them home.

Renewal, I believe, is for the Church, but what God is doing will eventually reach the lost. Healthy church growth occurs not from "migrating geese" but from a steady influx of new believers coming into the Kingdom. Do not be discouraged if the renewal does not produce growth. I do not believe it was intended to. Perhaps the coming harvest will.

Resist The Devil

As you humble yourself like a child, continue stubbornly to believe in God's grace. So what if you do not have enough faith? Your Heavenly Father does. Keep seeking Him. So what if you lose everything? Your Heavenly Father owns everything and will keep you. Staying receptive is a form of resisting the devil.

As your spirit is refreshed, you will find those habits of thinking that caused you to succumb quickly to temptation, no longer a habit. It is not a matter of fleshly effort and repeating Scriptures over and over with a sense of emptiness, but of refusing to indulge the luxury of depression.

Keep Believing In The River Of God's Spirit

Many did not recognize Jesus as the Messiah when He came, but to those who did, He became the most precious relationship in life. Even in her grief and despair, Mary Magdalene made her way to the tomb and was there to see Him risen from the dead.

There may be times you do not feel like going on. But keep going back to him, even if no one else does. God will provide you with places and ways to receive the necessary touch in your spirit. Recognize your Source of oil.

Guard The Temple Of The Holy Spirit

Charles Finney identified one reason for the dissipation of revival: that the overeager abandoned reasonable attention to ordinary physical needs. You cannot *feel* (which is essential to receiving and maintaining revival) when you are tired:

> Multitudes of Christians commit a great mistake here in time of revival. They are so thoughtless, and have so little judgment that they will break up their habits of living, neglect to eat and sleep at the proper hours, and let the excitement run away with them, so that they over do their bodies, and are so imprudent that they soon become exhausted, and it is impossible for them to continue in the work. Revivals often cease from negligence and imprudence, in this respect, on the part of those engaged in carrying them on, and declensions follow. *Finney on Revival,* pp. 62-63

While the apathetic may seize on the necessity of sufficient rest to support their laziness, those who need to hear it are those most on fire. Avoid drawing any conclusions about the status of your heart or about the renewal in general when you are tired. A good night's sleep may be all you and your church friends need to rekindle the flame.

Members of the church in Toronto were urged not to attend more than three renewal meetings per week when they were conducting nightly meetings, but to go also to their small groups, to maintain fellowship with others in their congregation.

We realized in our own congregation that we could not sustain nightly meetings several times per week. Instead, we opted for opening our regular service to renewal, praying for everyone wanting prayer at each service. In May 1996, John and Carol Arnott came to a renewal conference our congregation sponsored. We wound up having to engage a large venue for the two nights of meetings. Afterward, we began weekly Friday night renewal meetings as well as monthly renewal weekends. If there are other congregations in your area who are embracing the outpouring, partner with them periodically to pour out the blessing on the community. It works as long as the individual congregations do not engage in a "tug of war" over believers attending the meetings and use them to try to build their own congregations.

While we are on the subject of guarding ourselves, there is the problem of "habituation." Habituation occurs when we "get used" to something and lose the ability to experience awe over it. I can only imagine what would have happened had the folks in the congregation in Toronto allowed "habituation" to determine whether or not they continued holding meetings. Bill and I did not arrive until eleven months after the Holy Spirit came to them on January 20, 1994. I am so glad they waited for me. In fact, the church in Toronto carried on with renewal meetings for more than a decade to accommodate the flow of seekers!

One day a few years afterward, I remember John Arnott asking a group of us pastors how long we thought Toronto should continue holding renewal meetings. I remember the Holy Spirit showing me a picture of Moses holding his rod over the Red Sea until all of Israel crossed on the dry land to continue the journey to the Promised Land. Only God knows the moment when everyone you are intended to bless has "crossed over." God began it and He will complete the work. Indeed, some of our most precious friends made their first trip to Toronto AFTER 2000, six years or more after the original outpouring. What if they had stopped? How many relationships would we not have made and how many weary Christians would not have been renewed?

Establish Personal Boundaries

In the parable of the ten virgins (Matthew 25), Jesus admonished the wise to guard their oil from the foolish. We cannot find our way to intimacy with the Lord, and eventually to the marriage supper of the Lamb, if we allow others—-even others who look like serious seekers— to drain us of our joy.

In order to stay on fire for Jesus in a dark hour, when the sleeping bride will be roused from slumber, she must keep her lamp filled with precious oil to light her way to the wedding. But others around —-sometimes those who are closest to you, those who want ministry from you constantly—will try to entice you into pouring your oil into their lamps when what you have been given is for you. It is their responsibility to find their way to the "dealers" and purchase it themselves. But if you are unable to establish proper boundaries, if you do not know the limits of true and false obligation, you may pour out what is meant for you, and later find yourself dry in your hour of need.

The only way the wise virgins could ensure that they had enough oil was to say no to the foolish virgins and exhort them to go buy a supply of oil for their own lamps. Unfortunately, it was too late. For this reason, it is vital to be aware of the River and to be refreshed by it when it is flowing.

I often wonder whether this River is the beginning of the harvest, or the the season Jesus was speaking about just before He comes again, when the virgins rise and trim their lamps. Is it time to buy the oil we need to fire our own lamps, our passion for Jesus? I believe the many signs of revival in the Church are alerting us to this precious season when the "oil store" is open and the wise can replenish their lamps.

After our lamps are filled, there may come a dark season in which we are tempted to fall asleep and our lamps will go out, a time when "most people's love will grow cold." (Matthew 24:12) I hope not. But we are being entrusted as stewards of oil that must be guarded, even to the point of seeming harsh and unloving. This means learning to place boundaries around your own supply and discerning the difference between those who will receive from the Holy Spirit themselves and those who only want to have what you have as cheaply as possible, with no cost to themselves.

Jesus exhorted us not to be judgmental, but He also urged us to refrain from casting our pearls, the treasures of His Kingdom, before swine-those who scorn the pearls - "and turn and tear you to pieces." (Matthew 7:6) Those who despise what God is doing, or who love to see you as disheartened as they are, resemble the birds of the air in Jesus' parable of the sower. (Mark 4)

Hold your treasures in your heart until you find someone who really needs and wants Jesus. Then let the Holy Spirit give you the cue to share your treasure. In those cases, as you give it away, your supply will be miraculously replenished.

Use Spiritual Weapons

Having the right heart is more than half the battle, but there comes a time to stand. This includes resisting the temptation to sin. Isaiah 55:7 says,

> Let the wicked forsake his way, and the unrighteousness man his thoughts; and let him return to the Lord, and He will have compassion on him; and to our God, for He will abundantly pardon.

Allow the Holy Spirit to keep restoring to you the blessing of a pure heart. Bc quick to confess sin and turn from it. If you are in doubt about whether to confess a sin to someone else, perhaps you should check with your pastor. Sometimes you can do great harm to another person. At other times, confession brings closure and reconciliation. To keep sinning and trying to receive the benefits of revival does not work. It will not be long before the Holy Spirit convicts you. If you do not surrender, you will find yourself feeling like withdrawing from the Lord and His Church.

But this is a day when God is calling prodigals to return, a day when we need to forgive ourselves and others for wrongdoing. The ability to forgive is one of the most powerful spiritual weapons in the arsenal. Jesus thought so much of the ability to forgive that He imparted it to His disciples in the Upper Room the very evening after His resurrection.

Perhaps you need the same impartation. Ask the Lord to breathe on you the ability to let go of hurts and sins committed against you by others. This will keep the ground broken up in your heart so that you can continue receiving the blessings of renewal. To refuse to forgive others hardens your heart. And until you let go of anger, hurts and bitterness, revival will come to a grinding halt in your life. Is what others have done against you worth the price of missing your day of visitation and the new filling of the Holy Spirit the Lord wants to give you?

But with a cleansed, forgiving heart, you will be able to wield the weapon of intercessory prayer with sincerity. When the enemy seems to encroach on your joy, rather than find fault, begin to pray. The pure, praying heart can destroy the works of the devil and sustain the blessing. Also, support your congregation and its leaders with positive prayers and Christian love that "covers a multitude of sins." (I Peter 4:8) Imagine how you would feel in a place of awesome responsibility knowing that others were praying for you!

Learning to guard the treasure of this renewal is vital to sustaining it. Preparing to contain the blessing is necessary to enjoying the benefits of it as long as the Lord wants you to.

But there is another, more insidious way of quenching the Holy Spirit. Before the next move of the Holy Spirit, we need to talk about it. Otherwise, we will repeat the mistakes of the past and put out the Holy Spirit's fire!

11 - UH-OH

Things were going so well, when in December of 1995, John Wimber flew to Toronto to meet with its leaders and ousted the Toronto church from the Association of Vineyard Churches. He did not like them using "catchers" when people received prayer. He also objected to what he thought was an undue emphasis on manifestations. He particularly objected to "exotic animal noises" which he thought Toronto was advocating.

One had only to spend time in the services in Toronto to realize this was an extreme reaction to what was actually happening. The prayer ministry at the end of every service was a time when the congregation permitted an unusual atmosphere of freedom. People were laughing, wailing, shouting and giving themselves to joy of the Holy Spirit. Who knows whether every one of the more than three million people who came to Toronto during the outpouring was manifesting purely the work of the Holy Spirit? In my opinion, John Wimber made a mistake in dismissing Toronto. They loved the Vineyard and were happy to be a part of it.

People surmised that Vineyard leaders who were close to Wimber, carried a negative report to him, and that John Wimber who had been dealing with grave illness personally and in his immediate family, relied too heavily on exaggerated reports. It is also possible that the true motive was more sinister. Was it a power play to remove John Arnott from the line of succession as the eventual leader of the Vineyard. Who knows and who cares?

There was no excuse to cut off fellowship and disown an entire group which actually had its birth in the Vineyard and its values. They just repeated the pattern common to every move of God wherein the parent organization disfellowships the progeny for some reason that later on seems very trivial. Such organizations do not operate like the Kingdom of Heaven but more like the kingdom of this world and cause the flow of life to diminish.

Jesus wants us to fellowship together as one body and has called us and placed in us a deep desire to love one another and to be together; but building according to our natural understanding creates a monster, a tomb for Christianity, out of which Jesus "escapes" in the form of a new revival. In his book, 2000 YEARS OF CHARISMATIC CHRISTIANITY, Dr. Eddie Hyatt also explores this phenomenon and its effects on the body of Christ. In certain periods of church history, the River has gone underground, but it has always kept flowing. It has flowed in small groups and fellowships that were often persecuted by the "mainstream," a misnomer because very often "mainstream" looks like life, but it is out of the Divine flow and is a large puddle of old water which is bound for eventual stagnation. It bears the "manmade" stamp that causes it to be vulnerable to becoming apostate.

The Methodist denomination is only one of many examples. Large sections of the denomination no longer ascribe to what its founder, John Wesley, believed and taught, but they have compromised the teachings of Jesus and have substituted progressivism and artificial social justice for the reality of genuine agape love. Large sections of the Methodist denomination do not even ascribe to the Bible as being the divinely inspired word of God and no longer believe in being "born again," which was one of Wesley's major themes. How could this happen? Had Wesley only known what he was creating and how it would devolve!

No one can build anything to contain the real God, nor immortalize what God has done, not a building nor an organization. Our structures are self-limiting. We cannot see far enough into the future to see what God is going to do next. Jonathan Edwards, for example, could not see far enough to realize that the Lord would restore the powerful gifts of the Holy Spirit to the Church in the twentieth century with the Pentecostal revival, the Latter Rain movement and the Charismatic Renewal that touched every denomination. Every move of God tends to believe or at least act like it has "arrived." Only those who are humble and flexible enough can stretch enough to accommodate the "new thing" God does.

Therefore, the Catholics persecuted the followers of Luther who then persecuted the Anabaptists. The Anglicans went after the Methodists who then resisted what came later. The Pentecostals persecuted the Latter Rain revival. Many denominations persecuted Charismatics many of whom then tried to form clubs identified with well-known teachers in the movement called the Discipleship movement. When that fell apart, Charismatics persecuted John Wimber and the Vineyard who then persecuted and excluded Toronto. Let's not do it again, please.

A true revival only dissipates when those affected begin to live once again out of the flesh and not the Spirit. No one wakes up and says to himself, "I am going to quench the Holy Spirit today." He is slowly seduced into it by his own selfish desires, some of which are based on fear and insecurity. These are in conflict with the Holy Spirit. One of those ways is trying to build something that the Holy Spirit doesn't want. When we quote Isaiah 55, "...For as the Heavens are higher than the earth, so are My ways higher than your ways and My thoughts higher than your thoughts," this includes how we "build" on what God has done. True revival is a magnificent work of the Holy Spirit, a true invasion of the Kingdom of God and only perpetuated by the fruit and the power of the Holy Spirit.

What is built by man, on the other hand, will have imitation, jealousy, selfish ambition and exclusivity as its building blocks and not the humble, supernatural touch of the Divine creator. Instead, man tends to build on the foundation God lays in revival with "wood, hay and stubble." It is usually a hierarchy which by its nature creates and promotes the temptation to be jealous and begin to strive to climb the hierarchy. It will have a factory smell to it because it is man generated and not God initiated. Our ideas of creativity have not much to do with originality but usually are no more than stretching the lines of things that already exist. We cannot make something never before seen out of nothing. Human beings reacting to God's moving produce similar results and not all reactions are godly, as in the case of Peter.

On the mount of transfiguration, Peter had the impulse to respond with what he thought was honor. With Jesus right there, he misinterpreted the vision he saw and thought that God wanted shrines to Jesus, Moses and Elijah! But Moses and Elijah's lives were only shadows of Christ, they are in no way His equal. Jesus is the Living God who cannot be honored by a building or any other structure. He came to establish His Kingdom and nothing else! Everything we do must have the values of the Kingdom of Heaven.

By the time 1994 arrived, I was burned out trying to do Jesus' work for Him. We went to Toronto looking for God's love which did not demand performance and adherence to a man-imposed standard, a problem we had observed nearly 20 years before this.

A Hard Lesson

We began our pastoral ministry in Pittsburgh in 1976. We had only been here a few months when the local superintendent of the denomination of which we were a part, the same denomination I grew up in, called my husband to a meeting. He told him that we needed to withdraw from the Charismatic renewal if we wanted to remain members in good standing of the denomination.

Although the local church congregations in that denomination were supposed to be autonomous and make decisions based on the scriptures, he believed that the scriptures we were alluding to were no longer applicable and that the gifts of the Holy Spirit were "for the first century and not for now." Now we had the Bible which the early church did not have and God was no longer available to do the supernatural works that He did in the early days of the Church in order to "get the ball rolling." He said to Bill that we were embracing doctrines that were espoused by ignorant people.

Bill said wryly, "You mean fishermen, like Peter...?"

This inflamed the man who reprimanded Bill in sanctimonious vibrato, "I couldn't be sorrier than if this had happened to my own son."

With that he took his "sword" and cut off all but $175/ month from our small salary subtracting a large supplement the denomination was giving us. If our congregation wanted to remain in the denomination, they would have to find a new pastor. This was at the time our daughter was about 9 months old. We had left Dallas a few months earlier, packed our belongings in a U-haul truck and made our way to Pittsburgh. We were living in a rough neighborhood in Pittsburgh and waiting for an outpouring of the Spirit which did not arrive until 18 years later.

I do not have time to elaborate here on the number of violations of the love of God this man's decision committed, but we decided then that we should just do as we felt the Lord had led us to do and remain where we were regardless of the cost. The congregation was comprised of people who had not been lifetime members of that denomination, and they did not like the denomination attempting to control the choice of pastor they had made, unanimously by the way.

Like He had in the destruction of the Tower of Babel (Genesis 11), God had put a "new tongue" in our mouths. We couldn't build with these folks any longer. God had done something "new" with us, and it separated us from them. It was not what we wanted, but through it, God delivered us from certain spiritual stagnation and the clutches of religion versus walking in the Spirit.

This sort of scenario has been played out on the stage of every sort of religious organization that exists today.That is why when I asked Dr. Eddie Hyatt (mentioned above), retired professor of church history at Christ for the Nations Institute, Dallas, TX, what causes revivals to stop. He said, "Institutionalization." So what is "institutionalization" and how does it stop revival?

Faulty Towers

Forming "clubs" is a pursuit I learned as a little girl with my playmates in the backyard. We would form "clubs" sometimes new ones on a daily basis. The first thing was an agenda to determine who was in and who was out. The reason we did this was because there was a natural human impulse to be exclusive. We wanted a defined boundary so we could more easily deal with pressing questions such as which dolls we were going to dress that day or which "secrets" we were going to divulge to each other.

In the wake of revival, believers also tend this way, much like the people who built the Tower of Babel. In Genesis 11, it says, "Now the whole earth spoke the same language and the same words. Upon realizing what they could accomplish together, they decided to build a city and a tower that would reach into heaven. They crafted man-made bricks and stuck them together with tar. The resulting edifice is commonly called the Tower of Babel. It even says that God came down to look at the tower which the sons of men had built. He did not like what He saw.

The architectural plan was based on man's idea of how to reach heaven- by climbing up. But humbling oneself is truly the only way to touch God. "I dwell in the high and holy place with him who is of a contrite and humble spirit, to revive the spirit of the meek and the heart of the contrite." (Isaiah 57:15) The builders of the Tower of Babel had an ambition to build something that would prevent them "being scattered about the face of the whole earth." When God took down the tower, He did it in such a way as to create the very thing they feared: being scattered throughout the face of the whole earth. He disrupted unity by causing them to speak different languages; they could no longer understand each other.

There are many justifications for establishing our own "faulty towers:" to belong to something tangible, to "protect" the members from unneeded exposure to errant doctrines or to further the ideals of the group. Underneath it is a very mixed motive and the breeding ground for works of the flesh whose foundational questions are as follows: who is in charge, how can we distinguish ourselves from the run-of-the-mill Christian, what about people who say they are from our group but who are not really? Who is going to keep the purity of our doctrine or bring discipline when it is needed? Then come the requirements for membership which always include money changing hands on some level.

The practice of forming "clubs" carries with it sins which must be committed in order to keep the wheels rolling. Why? Because it is a hierarchical incentive system built by perfectionism and performance orientation. It demands choices that should never be made by human beings- even Christian human beings. By its very nature it excludes. While they accuse non-participants of drawing to themselves; actually the opposite is the case. The club erects boundaries in the form of rules, non-negotiable requirements that mask themselves as being good, but are really tests of conformity. Now there is an "us" distinct from the rest of the body of Christ. Usually the powers-that-be form "seminaries" or "schools" to train believers in the "club" ideals. Then the people who want to remain "in good standing" will follow the arbitrary guidelines imposed by the hierarchy's decisions. If one is unable to follow the guidelines, they are then "out." These mandatory requirements do not coincide with scripture although they will claim to originate from scripture. If someone doesn't join in, they are "rebellious" and "independent" minded. There are always consequences to non-participation because you have now proven your unwillingness to recognize "authority" and submit to it.

Historically, it has often been true that at this point women are excluded from leadership because they are unable to attend the training schools as they must be home with the kids. In order to remain "in good standing," you must ascribe to the "look alike, think alike" mentality so that if some individual from some-where else is looking to fellowship with "our club" they will im-mediately recognize it because we all do the same things in the same way.

The primary focus is no longer about one's relationship with Jesus. That is only secondary. It is all about the "club." In the past, these "clubs" have gone by various names, such as denom-inations, ministry fellowships, cells or now, "tribes." While it seems harmless, it is one of the main quenchers of a genuine move of the Holy Spirit because what was once a free-flowing move of the Holy Spirit has taken on characteristics of organiza-tion that lead to the formation of a well-oiled machine which is able to run regardless of whether or not God's presence is actu-ally there. All it needs to function is recruiting new "fodder." The Apostle Paul warned the Church about this in I Corinthians 3 -4. He cautioned believers against "arrogance" which was at the root of it.

As the decades wander on, repetitiveness becomes tradition and the clinging to the established ideals erodes the possibility of change, but worst of all, it erodes the Lordship of Jesus Christ and substitutes "letter" in its place. It happened in the first cen-tury as Roman Catholicism and orthodoxy formed around the glow of the original revival so that by the 300's, the original teachings of Jesus were corrupted and overlaid with the cello-phane wrappings of ritual and form. The church has been in slow recovery ever since.

An institution, like a prison, takes away freedom but replaces it with three meals a day and a bunk or in this case, the illusion of "belonging" and often, in our day in America, a group health insurance plan. Prison is an artificial, dysfunctional community which attempts to rehabilitate inmates by the letter of the law. There is no love there, outside those guards and inmates who have come to Jesus and live according the law of love. The way a prison functions adds new meaning to the word, "legalism." Curiously, if a person becomes institutionalized, he reaches a moment where he is unable to function outside the institution. The comfortable sameness, albeit hellish, supplants the privilege of freedom.

So then the problem is not only the organization itself but the motive behind its establishment. It is not out of genuine love and concern for those involved. It is doomed to have an artificial life and any approval is contingent upon the whims of the hierarchy. It leverages relationship that should be given unconditionally out of pure motives.

The More Excellent Way

When the denomination issued that ultimatum: leave or deny the experience of the baptism in the Holy Spirit, we had to leave or deny the reality of what the Lord had done in our lives, we had no choice. Nevertheless, the years from 1981 until 1995 were years when an elderly pastor named A.J. Rowden from Kansas City, MO took us under his wing. With Pastor Rowden, you never signed anything, and he never gave input unless we invited him to which happened often. There was something in Pastor Rowden that made you want to stand up and salute. He never indicated in any way that he wanted such respect, but I suppose it was the genuine anointing of the Holy Spirit. He was kind to us. He had been drummed out of the Evangelical United Brethren over the same issue decades before and knew what it was like. Pastor Rowden's congregation sponsored two pastors' conferences a year which Bill and I began to attend regularly. Pastor Rowden was opposed to "capturing" church congregations to build a formal ministry fellowship or denomination. With them, everything was free, no strings attached. There was no cost to their conferences. If we would just make our way there, their congregation paid for the hotel and prepared two meals/day for the 4 days of the convention. Pastors and their spouses from churches all over the midwestern United States made their way twice a year to enjoy a respite and a time of honor which they were so often denied by those in their own congregations.

Pastor Rowden would often come up to couples sitting in the congregation who were in ministry, place his hands on their shoulders and give them words of blessing and comfort. His words cut through all the wounds of ministry and surrounded your spirit with the love of God, the Father. In 1995, right after the renewal began, Pastor Rowden began to experience cognitive decline; but he was so full of the Spirit that he actually confirmed his own words of prophecy by praying prophetically over you one day and then praying prophetically the same word over you the next day! We owe much of the foundation that has been laid in us to Pastor Rowden. He seemed so content to be who he was without fanfare. He was an encourager who saw his role as a servant, not a king.

One of the last memories we have of Pastor Rowden was of him standing on the platform, tapping his cane in time to the music as his congregation enjoyed the experience of a "fire tunnel." He transitioned into the new move, as he was able to do with every one in his lifetime, because he recognized God in it.

He lived to be well into his 90's and passed away in a nursing home. His daughter, Roberta, said that the weekend before he died, she visited him and they sang together and worshipped the Lord. Pastor Rowden nurtured in us a very deep hunger for revival, because he saw it as a necessary part of God's plan for restoring the Church. Pastor Rowden often said that the Lord would build His Church.

When we would ask for advice, he would say, " Well, I remember when that happened to me..." Instead of telling us what to do, he would say, "Do whatever the Lord tells you to do." He admonished us that in revivals, people tend toward extremes of doctrine and practice. There is a cost to staying in the flow: keeping Jesus as the center of the Church's focus and loving one another.

However, had we been linked with the former denomination, we would not have been able to know him because we would have been confined to fellowshipping with only people of that denomination. Pastor Rowden was able to escape the trap of institutionalization and was able to transition from one move of the Spirit to another because he remained humble and teachable.

During revival, God breaks walls that men build up. As our Episcopalian friend, Joanne Stockhowe, said about the early days of the Charismatic Movement, "The water rose above the walls, and we were all swimming in the same River. But gradually as the tide receded, everyone sank back into their old denominational ways." Fellowship across denominational lines dwindled significantly and fear of one another and the longing for the "safety" of our denominational languages took over once again.

What if we left the protection of the revival's values up to God? What if we refused to climb the hierarchy? What if we left fellowship up to the Holy Spirit's leading? What if we fellowshipped together without any other agenda than loving God and each other? What if you keep soaking?Are there indeed any "toxic levels" of the Holy Spirit?

You Can Try This At Home

There are fellowships like this that started out of the Toronto outpouring. One of them is the River Center on the outskirts of Fort Worth, TX. For over 26 years, it has met in the home of Bob and Cindy Parton. When Cindy encountered the "blessing," it was in the beginning in 1994, when the Arnotts first went to the Dallas-Fort Worth area. Carol Arnott taught a workshop on "soaking" in God's presence and challenged people to do it at home. Bob and Cindy wanted more and so it began.

Their house on a corner in North Richland Hills, TX became a place where the hungry and thirsty for more of Jesus could find Him again. Every Monday night their house was packed with hungry people from all over the metroplex and even as far away as Oklahoma and Texarkana. Folks from Houston came, a five-hour drive away! To date, people have come from all over the

US and from other places in the world to their living room to "soak" in the presence of God. They are not focused on numbers or money. In fact, they rarely receive a formal "offering." Their group is called the River Center. It is more like the early church than 99 per cent of the congregations I've been to, and it is still going strong, keeping the fire lit!

Bob and Cindy give the agenda over to the Holy Spirit. They start around 7 on Monday nights with whoever comes lying on the floor with pillows and blankets listening to Christian music and focusing quietly on Jesus. After about a half hour, the facilitator, usually Bob or Cindy, asks, "Does anyone have something they have received that they would like to share?" Then people tell what scriptures came to mind and even what mental impressions they are receiving. The gifts of the Holy Spirit begin to flow. They allow the Lord to speak through the ones He chooses. Sometimes, they invite a guest speaker who only shares after the people share what the Holy Spirit has given them.

Recently, one young woman shared an insight she received. A newcomer was amazed at the depth and ease with which she shared. She asked the young woman why she could be sharing at such a deep level considering her young age. The young woman replied, "No, I've just been soaking here for 18 years, since I was three years old. " She had so developed her ability to listen to God's voice and prized Him because He has always been the central focus of the meetings.

Bob and Cindy are faithful to the light they have received, and they have withstood the test of time. They will be among those who "shine like the stars in the firmament" (Daniel 12:3) because they have led many to righteousness without coveting a position or a name for themselves. They are a gift to the body of Christ because they are genuine fire keepers.

"Behold, How They Love One Another"

The true mark of God-initiated fellowship is not found in perfect doctrine or sophisticated organization. When the Holy Spirit pours Himself out, the chief evidence is found in genuine love of one another. None of us may live to see "the end of all things." Perhaps it doesn't matter whether we die in the Great Tribulation or a mini-tribulation. All that will matter is whether or not we knew that God the Father loved us enough to cause us to genuinely love one another. And love does not institutionalize well.

12 - FROM THE RIVER TO THE ENDS OF THE EARTH

As large numbers of people began to experience the blessing in many countries of the world, people began to ask, 'Where is this going?' 'What now?'

Perhaps it is good to remember what Jesus said, "Take no thought for tomorrow." (Matthew 6:24) We do not live in tomorrow, we are alive today. Indeed, almost three decades on, I can honestly answer that the Toronto Blessing was the last genuine move of the Holy Spirit that some people were able to experience. So many people, even ones mentioned in this book, have died.

My husband and I were eating lunch one Sunday at a restaurant in Pensacola during the late '90's. A family was sitting in a booth next to us separated only by a lattice partition and a few plants. They overheard us talking about what was happening at the revival meetings in Pensacola and Toronto. After we ate, the man from the booth next to us approached my husband and said, "I couldn't help overhearing you talking about revivals. My pastor says that it's no big deal. These things come around every twenty years or so, so we don't need to get so excited."

Bill said to him, looking at his white hair. Pointing to his own gray crown of glory, Bill said, "Well, judging from your hair and mine, we may not have that long to wait; maybe we should not ignore what God has sent today."

In the book of Ezekiel, the prophet shared that he saw a river flowing from the temple into the land around it until it reached the Dead Sea. The Dead Sea is famous for not harboring any life because of its high saline content. It is so salty that one can sit in it and not sink. In his vision, Ezekiel observed the places where the River flowed and said:

> Every living creature which swarms in every place where the river goes will live. And there will be many fish, for these waters go there, and the others become fresh; so everything will live where the river goes. (Ezekiel 47:9)

What Ezekiel saw was the river of God's Spirit flowing into a sea of corrupt, spiritually dead humanity and restoring it with life-giving water from the presence of God. The apostle John, late in his life, saw the source of the same river that Ezekiel saw—the river flowing from the throne of God in Heaven, bordered as Ezekiel saw it; with trees whose leaves were for the healing of the nations. (Revelation 22:1-2; Ezekiel 47:12) Ezekiel also saw fishermen along the banks of what was once the Dead Sea, casting nets and gathering in fish. What began as water trickling out of the house of God turned into an end-time harvest of souls.

This river of life has the power to revive from the dead! God could have had the river flow directly from His throne. Instead, He caused it to flow through the house of of the Lord. Today this is the body of Christ, people who worship Jesus from every people, tongue, tribe and nation on the face of the earth. Jesus promised that "he who believes in Me as the Scripture said, from his innermost being shall flow rivers of living water." (John 7:38) The refreshing power of the Holy Spirit only needs a way out of the church's walls into the world.

John Arnott was speaking to a pastors gathering at our congregation in 1998. One of the pastors there asked him, "When does renewal become revival?"

Without hesitation, John answered, "When you open your mouth."

God is looking for believers who will not capture the blessing for themselves and their congregations, but for people who will release the life giving flow into the world around them. The move of the Holy Spirit is not a "parlor game" where we pray for each other constantly without regard to the spiritually dead outside the church.

"From The River To The Ends Of The Earth..."

Until I worked with believers from Canada, I did not know that the founders of Canada chose Psalm 72:8 as their founding scripture. "...May He have dominion from sea to sea and from the River to the ends of the earth." I am not sure what River the psalmist was referring to, but I believe the Lord did. It is not just ironic, it is prophetic. The River that sprang up in Canada flowed to the ends of the earth and continues to water the thirsty ground.

There is no more thirsty ground than the Middle East. The ancient home of the patriarchs is crying out as Isaiah promised for "waters in the wilderness and Rivers in the desert." Although Isaac and Ishmael are still at war, God is no respecter of persons. He loves them all.

Our friend, Tino DiSienna, is a pastor in Queens, NY. On one of his trips to Toronto, he took along his friend, Joe Gregorian, an Armenian immigrant from Iran, who immigrated to America in the '70's as the shah was deposed and the ayatollahs took power and quashed religious freedom. Joe's dry-humored line, "I ran from I-ran" always makes me chuckle.

As Joe received prayer in Toronto, he fell to the carpet under the power of the Holy Spirit. Immediately, he became aware of the Iranians who were in need of the Gospel of Jesus Christ. He "saw" an outline of the map of Iran. Joe and his wife, Anna, took this as a direct command from the Lord to reach out to Iranians through the Internet.

They began communicating in Farsi online with people who were becoming dissatisfied with Islam and looking for the real

God. Their message was the love of God in sending His son, Jesus Christ, to redeem them. To their amazement, the Holy Spirit was already busy there creating deep thirst among Iranians to know Him. They were having dreams and visions where Jesus appeared to them. As a direct result of the refreshing power of the Holy Spirit, Joe and Anna reached out from their living room in New Jersey and led Iranians to Christ. They began to disciple them sending them Bibles and linking them together to form congregations. It was good that Joe acted on that word because sadly he passed away in March 2021.

Another couple who went to Toronto for the first time in 2000, must remain anonymous because they are secretly "on the field." They have been there for about 2 decades now teaching in one of the universities in an Islamic country which strictly forbids preaching Jesus Christ. They were there when Mel Gibson released his epic movie, "The Passion of the Christ."

They were there at the first showing. At the end of the movie, there was silence—-except for quiet sobbing. At the university where he teaches the next day, students who had also seen the movie were full of questions. "What was that giant teardrop falling from heaven...?" "Why was Satan enraged when Jesus died?..."Because they asked, he was able to share why the love of God motivated Him to send His Son to redeem those who are lost.

Not long ago, I read an article about the "revival" in Iran. Christianity is now the fastest growing "religion" there. Many home fellowships are springing up, meeting secretly to avoid detection by the Islamic fundamentalist regime. The majority of the pastors are women whose lives have been transformed by hope they now have in Jesus Christ. This powerful phenomenon gives new understanding to the scripture, "In Christ there is neither Jew nor Greek, male nor female, slave or free for you are all one in Christ Jesus." (Galatians 3: 27-28)

When our Heavenly Father looks at every region of the world, I believe He sees not individual "churches" or even denominations, but He sees one supernatural Church composed of His children who are "born from above." (...the Lord knows them that are His. 2 Timothy 2:19) Bill and I have stopped referring to the congregation we serve as pastors as a "church." We are really serving a congregation of believers who are loving and serving one another. The word "Church," in my opinion, should be reserved for the body the way God sees it.

In Pittsburgh in 1997, during the early days of the outpouring we met for several weeks with two other congregations who had responded favorably to the new move of God. The meetings we had together caused the spread of the power of the Holy Spirit to hundreds of people who would have never been exposed to it.

Stuart Bell and several other people from England and other places in the body of Christ ministered at those meetings. The power of God manifested in the same way as we had seen Him do in meetings in Toronto. It was as though God could not wait to get His hands on the people in Pittsburgh.

After the meetings, our congregation continued to hold weekly renewal meetings for over ten years. The Lord saturated us and blessed us as we freely gave away the blessing. As walls began to break, we flowed together in the same River of blessing. A few months into it, one of the congregations we met with received an offering for our congregation, enough money to replace the carpet in our sanctuary. For several years we met together with other pastors to pray together and fellowship as a result of how the Holy Spirit was moving among us.

Unity cannot be achieved by man's efforts, only by common experience in the Holy Spirit. When God moves to create it, man sustains it by releasing the selfless love of God. The body of Christ today looks very little like the Church in the first century. It is professional, sometimes driven by the values of the world, insuring that individual congregations vie for prominence through goals such as size and budget. However, when revival comes, the values of the Kingdom replace the worldly values that have crept in and all but completely swallowed the goal of simplicity and purity of devotion to Christ.

This has the effect of "leveling" the playing field. The world's values and the values of the Kingdom don't mix. When the values of the world are in place, jealousy and selfish ambition take over and men "rule." But when true revival comes, God goes for the simple in order to highlight the fact that He hasn't changed His mind about who is the "greatest in the Kingdom of Heaven."

Will There Be Another Wave?

God spoke to Jeremiah, "..if you extract the precious from the worthless, then you will become my spokesman."

What is truly precious in revival is the spiritual reality of firing one's passion for Jesus and your relationship to Him, the revelation that the Father loves you and that the Holy Spirit is present to form the genuine motivation for life and its pursuits. As the years pass, as friends go by the way and the current atmosphere replaces its atmosphere, the white hot fire tends to dissipate as the cluster of affected people scatters. What will you retain from what God has done in your life?

What has remained with me is a fire that has not gone out. We have endured severe trials including unwanted separation from friends through death, geographical and ideological differences. Yet we have a host of friends all over the world who can testify that what happened to them as a result of what God did in Toronto beginning in 1994 and beyond remains in them. When one tries to define the purpose of it, it is best embodied in the personal testimonies of each one affected by it. It was a major turning point in their spiritual growth and maturity.

One day early in the days of the Toronto outpouring, I was standing beside the copier in our own church office. Suddenly, I "knew" that there is going to be another GREAT AWAKENING. Today, I see that this time it will occur worldwide and with a far greater effect than anything we have previously experienced. News of it will partially be spread by electronic media, but it will occur spontaneously in countries that are widely separated by geographical, cultural and language barriers. It will create genuine unity of the Holy Spirit and will be centered on Jesus. It will cause a dramatic change in the Church and will sound a trumpet gathering people to Christ in an unprecedented flood. There will be joy and a wave of holiness that will cause a drastic separation between genuine Christians and those who are so in label only. The Church will once again spurn the methods of the flesh and submit to the values of His Kingdom. There will be signs and wonders. There will be division and persecution, but evil will be drawn out into the open and become the object of disdain. The Church will know what has robbed her of love and will be consecrated to Her Lord.

So how do you prepare for what God does next? Keep loving anyway and hold fast what the Lord gives you. He has come with a higher purpose than you can imagine. Let go into the flow of His love because underneath everything you can see with your eyes, the River is still here, and He will not leave you or forsake you. Humble yourself, take the lower seat, do not strive but wait patiently and He will bring it to pass in His good time.

What About Me Right Now?

What if revival is nowhere near me? What if I honestly can't get there? What if I'm reading this decades after the 1994 outpouring? Can God move on me out of "season?"

Jesus started His ministry in His hometown synagogue by saying, "There were many lepers in the time of Elisha, but none were healed except Namaan, the Syrian…" Luke 4:27. If reading this book has ignited in you a spark, it is God wanting to give you more of Himself. Humble yourself right now. Ask God to pour out His Spirit on you and to even refill you if you have become dry. God's blessings are never limited to the "seasons" of man. He is timeless. To Him 1994 is the same as today! He is ready for you, if you are truly ready for Him. Lift your "cup" to Him and pray, "Come, Holy Spirit! I can't live without your love one more moment. Fill me, please, with a fresh baptism of your fire!"

This River will never dry up because its source is the eternal Holy Spirit. It flows until it merges with other tributaries and creates a greater River as with the Mississippi River in the US which flows from tributaries in the Rocky Mountains and the Alleghenies of Pennsylvania and creeks and the lakes of Minnesota until it reaches the Gulf of Mexico at New Orleans. By the time it reaches New Orleans, the droplets do not bear the marks of the tributary from whence they came but are indistinguishable from each other and are known only as the Mississippi. The River of God is the same, flowing from the headwaters of heaven, it flows through history and the generations of people who have allowed the Holy Spirit to flow through them to water the earth with the Gospel of Jesus Christ. The River will be visible as long as God remains in control. Its life giving flow will resurrect the dead and renew the dormant. The challenge is to not dam it up or pollute it so that what God intends for it is accomplished.

What is truly precious in revival is the spiritual reality of firing one's passion for Jesus and your relationship to Him, the revelation that the Father loves you and that the Holy Spirit is present to form the genuine motivation for life and its pursuits. As the years pass, as friends go by the way and the current atmosphere replaces its atmosphere, the white hot fire tends to dissipate as the cluster of affected people scatters. What will you retain from what God has done in your life?

What has remained with me is a fire that has not gone out. We have endured severe trials including unwanted separation from friends through death and ideological differences. Yet we have a host of friends all over the world who can testify that what happened to them as a result of what God did in Toronto beginning in 1994 remains in them. When one tries to define the purpose of it, it is best embodied in the personal testimonies of each one affected by it. It was a major turning point in their spiritual growth and maturity.

For me, this has been the most precious Divine moment in all my life, a fresh baptism in His river of fire. It was the day when God fulfilled prophetic word to us, "Behold, I will do something new...I will even make a roadway in the wilderness and rivers in the desert." (Isaiah 43: 18-21) It was a time when I began to allow God to love me. Before it, I could feel very little, but since His touch on my life in this period of revival I am awake now with a love for Jesus I can feel. I like to say, 'Is it renewal or revival?— It depends on how dead you were when it started.' For me, it was and is revival!

Printed in Great Britain
by Amazon

69174585R00119